Praise for *F*

'A jocular and candid account of the extraordinary culture of Japan through the wide eyes of an adventurous, and at times hapless, westerner. Essential reading for student teachers, backpackers and Japanophiles.'
Ginny Light, former online travel editor, **The Times**

'I thoroughly enjoyed *For Fukui's Sake*. It really evokes that excitement of 'discovering' Japan for the first time. Baldwin's sheer love of the country and its people comes across, while [he] acknowledges that it's not always easy being a foreigner there. Made me want to get on a plane and go straight back to Japan.'
Jan Dodd, co-author, **Rough Guide to Japan**

'A fascinating journey and a call to action for anyone stuck in a boring job who secretly dreams of escaping overseas.'
Mark Hodson, travel writer, **The Sunday Times**

'A witty and highly entertaining account of a hapless Englishman's experience of teaching in rural Japan, where the cultural chasms between the two countries provide for some hilarious moments. A fascinating insight into the lives of ordinary Japanese people.'
Helen Arnold, author, **1001 Escapes To Make Before You Die**

'If you've ever idly dreamed of a new life abroad, Baldwin's Japanese adventure might just get you packing. From that first chopstick-full of octopus, to sharing a sunrise on Fuji, *For Fukui's Sake* is an honest account of cultural discovery and friendship, and a lesson in the rewards of stepping outside your comfort zone.'
Ed Blomfield, editor, **Whitelines Magazine**

'An enchanting and surprising story [of life] in a part of Japan few get to experience. Told with humour and elegance.'

Jennifer Barclay, author, ***Meeting Mr Kim***

'I've been a frequent visitor to Japan, but Baldwin's fascinating book reveals a much deeper insight into Japanese culture than I have ever managed to discover. He saw his time there as a year in – not a year out. A great read.'

Arnie Wilson, ski travel writer, ***The Financial Times***

'Brought back happy memories of my visit [to Japan] and added a whole lot more I hadn't realised. Reading about the real experience is much more valuable than any guide book; this book makes doing so a pleasure.'

Patrick Thorne, ski travel writer, ***The Independent on Sunday***

'The Japanese are often labelled 'inscrutable' [but] Baldwin managed to penetrate that veneer during his experience of living and working in a rural community in Japan. Amusing and revealing, [he] transports the reader to his side.'

Ken Forman, treasurer, ***Japan Society of Scotland***

For Fukui's Sake
Two years in rural Japan

By Sam Baldwin

Baka Books

Copyright © Sam Baldwin 2011

First published 2011

The moral right of Sam Baldwin to be identified as the author of this work has been asserted by him in accordance with the Copyright, Designs and Patents Act of 1988.

All rights reserved. No part of this publication may be reproduced, stored in a retrieval system or transmitted in any forms or by any means, electronic, mechanical, photocopying, recording or otherwise, without the prior permission of both the copyright owner and the publisher of this book.

Cover illustration and map by James Ferguson.

Published by Baka Books, printed on demand by CreateSpace.

ISBN: 978-1467924146

For more information visit:
ForFukuisSake.com

About the Author

Sam Baldwin has written about travel for *The Guardian*, *The Times*, *The Independent* and *The Scotsman*, and has contributed to numerous magazines and guide books. He now lives in Edinburgh where he works as an editor and writer for a large online travel company.

About the Book

For Fukui's Sake is the true account of two years spent living and working as an English teacher in the small, backcountry town of Ono, Fukui, Japan. Some of the timelines have been condensed, some of the experiences consolidated, and some of the names have been changed, but everything recounted actually happened.

For more information visit:
ForFukuisSake.com

Contents

Prologue

1. The Sensei has Landed
2. Journey to Fujisan
3. Lessons in Laughter
4. What Happens at the *Enkai* Stays at the *Enkai*
5. Teeth Wisdom
6. Animal Encounters
7. A Night at Yumeya
8. Green Tea and Cake with Keiko
9. Encapsulated
10. Adventures in Snow
11. Feeling Foreign in Fukui
12. Holy Snow on Hakusan
13. Tales of Tokyo
14. Cooling Off in the Kuzuryu
15. The Sock Smeller
16. Adrift on Obama Bay
17. Festival Fever
18. Slow Boat to Hokkaido
19. Of Samurai, Swords and Sushi
20. Creatures of the Kuzuryu
21. Confessions of a Failed *Taiko* Drummer
22. Sayonara Sadness

Epilogue

Acknowledgments

Map of Japan and Fukui

Prologue

When you walk into work every day only to ask yourself 'is this really *it?*', then it probably isn't.

But 'is this really *it?*' was what I found myself asking with increasing frequency as I slipped into my white lab coat and snapped on a pair of latex gloves each morning.

Officially, I was a 'Research Laboratory Technician'. I was pleased to have finally landed a job in science after months of admin work in grey government offices but in reality, I was closer to a cleaner than a scientist. My degree in Pharmacology wasn't exactly proving essential knowledge for spraying cell incubators with virus-killing chemicals or ferrying bags of used centrifuge tubes to the incinerator.

I was no stranger to mundane jobs; I'd done my time on factory production lines, worked 12-hour nightshifts in refrigerated warehouses and been a lowly dishwasher in a restaurant kitchen. I just thought that, by now, I'd have found my calling. But I hadn't and while my colleagues were getting excited about new research in the 'International Journal of Lower Extremity Wounds', I was losing more interest each day and finding it increasingly hard to feign enthusiasm for the science that surrounded me.

The months went on and I continued to perform the routine tasks that were required for a research lab to function smoothly but I was growing increasingly unhappy with the road my life seemed to be taking. My workmates were a friendly bunch and were doing great work for a noble cause but after just a few months, I knew that laboratory life was not for me. It was my boss who unwittingly triggered the panic that forced me to act.

'Sam, have you ever thought about your future here? You can earn good money as a lab technician and we offer great pensions and excellent health benefits.'

His words thrust me into a future where a slightly plumper, slightly balder Sam Baldwin in a white lab coat and latex gloves was still loading conical flasks into a dishwasher, still mixing up solutions of methanol, still weighing out microscopic amounts of powdered enzymes.

Surely this couldn't be *it*? Surely I couldn't spend the rest of my working days as a slave to the scientists, a lab-coated bin man, in exchange for an annual pay rise and a pension? I was having a mid-life crisis, about 20 years too early.

I made up my mind; I had to get out.

***

At school, in geography class, we had learned about 'push and pull factors'. These are the reasons why people move from one place to another. Japan had never been somewhere that I'd thought much about before but one day, a friend who had ventured there started sending me his stories of mountains and vast volumes of snow. I have never lost my child-like love of snow and have always yearned for more mountains, so it was exactly the pull factor I needed. His emails and pictures became a very welcome window into an intoxicating land and an escape from the push factor: my job.

I was soon spending all my spare minutes at work scouring the net for more information as I set my sights on the Japanese archipelago.

I applied, and was accepted, for a job as an assistant English language teacher on a programme run by the Japanese government. In April 2004, I nervously knocked on my boss' door to inform him that he would need to replace me.

Many of my colleagues seemed slightly suspicious of my intentions and were puzzled as to why anyone would want to leave a perfectly good career and go off on a whim to the other side of the world. Their most pressing concern was the question of how I would find employment upon my return:

'It sounds fun but what are you going to do when you get back?'
Others just saw my itchy feet as an ailment that needed to be cured: 'So you're taking a gap year? A year out? Do it while you can, get it out of your system.'

But I didn't see Japan as a year *out*. I saw it as a year *in*. I wanted to get it *into* my system and no, I didn't know what I was going to do when I got back, and I didn't care either. I knew there was more to life than microscopes and micropipettes; I knew there were more doors to open out there in the wide world; I just had to find those doors.

So after two years of playing a rather small part in the battle against cancer, I hung my lab coat on its peg and peeled off the latex gloves for the last time. I was leaving my job, friends and family to go and work as an English teacher in a remote, rural Japanese town. I had no teaching experience and sometimes had problems speaking English fluently, let alone Japanese. I was the kid who had pleaded with my parents not to send me on the French exchange. Now I was leaving voluntarily, and for a country far more foreign than France. But I needed a change and was ready to take a chance. So in July 2004, I took one last look over London as the plane wheeled away from the capital and soared towards Japan, where I hoped I might find something more.

And I did find more. The two-year adventure saw me tumble into love with a forgotten nook of Japan: a rural, sometimes wild land, encircled by mountains and patch-worked with paddies. It was a place where bears hunted humans, where the snow crushed houses and where foreigners were still considered curious creatures.

I would never return to the lab. Japan would ultimately change my career path completely, and as for those next two years, the question 'is this really *it*?' never once entered my mind.

Chapter 1
The Sensei has Landed

Sweat trickles down my temple as I'm led to the stage on an intensely hot and humid summer's day. I stand alone as I nervously scan the sea of black-haired people gazing up at me, the blue-eyed, big-nosed foreigner.

It's my first day at Kamisho Junior High, a small countryside school on the outskirts of Ono, Japan, and I'm about to give my introductory speech to the entire school, in Japanese. I glance down at my scribbled notes, hastily contrived with the help of my new best friend: a Japanese phrasebook.

My heart pounds. I don't speak the language and I'm petrified of public speaking in English, let alone Japanese. Why did I leave an easy job with a pension and 'excellent health benefits' to come here?

Suddenly, being the lab-coated bin man doesn't seem so bad after all.

***

Three months after my interview with the Japan Exchange and Teaching (JET) Programme – a government-run scheme that places English speakers in schools throughout Japan, from the tropical islands of Okinawa, to the sub-arctic isle of Hokkaido – an envelope from the Japanese Embassy arrived. I anxiously tore it open, scanned the document and saw the word 'Fukui'.

At first I thought it was an incredibly rude rejection letter. Then I realised it was a job offer and that 'Fukui' was actually a place. But where the Fukui was it? I made a dash for Google but my research was hampered by the fact that there was very little in English about this smallish, provincial and apparently rather rural prefecture, situated on the west coast of Honshu, and the scraps of information that I did eventually find weren't particularly encouraging.

'Little reason to linger here' was the conclusion of the traveller's bible, *The Rough Guide to Japan*. In his book *The Roads to Sata*, Alan Booth, who walked from Hokkaido to Kyushu in the early '80s and wrote of the journey was 'struck by the coarseness of Fukui manners' and left with a 'less than sunny impression' of the Fukui natives, having been taunted by kids and refused entry to numerous Japanese inns on account of his foreignness. The final piece of praise for Fukui came from Will Ferguson, author of the *Hokkaido Highway Blues*, who hitchhiked the length of the country in the '90s and wrote that Fukui was 'home to the rudest people in Japan', after he was left waiting for a lift in the pouring rain for several hours.

Further research revealed that Fukui prefecture had fifteen nuclear reactors, was a hot spot for fossilized dinosaurs and had a rare rock formation on the coast that was notorious for suicides. It was with these exciting endorsements in mind that I touched down in Tokyo during sauna-like August humidity, snowboard under arm, shirt fused to back, and cursed my bad luck at having been assigned to the small town of Ono, a rural backwater unheard of by most people, including the Japanese.

***

My first week in Japan was daunting and tiring but immensely exciting. Courtesy of the JET Programme, I was staying in the five-star Keio Plaza Hotel in central Tokyo with hundreds of other exhausted but elated new arrivals. Despite trying to convince them otherwise, my new roommates, Mike and Lewis, two fellow Englishmen also destined for Fukui, had announced that they were too tired to do anything other than sleep after the twelve-hour flight and had crawled into bed straight away. I was also in need of slumber but with all of Tokyo's steel, neon and glass waiting outside my window, there was no chance of rest now.

So after a quick shower and some experimentation with the toilet's computerised console, I stepped through the revolving door of the air conditioned hotel, into the thick, humid heat that is the Tokyo summer.

For the sleep-starved, wide-eyed westerner on his first ever visit to Japan's capital, there is far too much to take in. Instead of trying to, I just let the intense Tokyo experience wash over me like a hallucinogenic trip. I wander through a high-rise forest of concrete that cast long shadows over narrow backstreets. Wading through soupy air, I catch whiffs of ripe sewage. The owner of a steaming noodle stand calls for custom and vending machines sing Japanese songs at me. Hard-hatted workmen duck into sushi bars that advertise menus with perfect plastic replicas. High-heeled ladies totter past, hidden under clutches of designer shopping bags. Students hand packs of branded tissues to the passing human traffic and sweating *salarymen* disappear into Tokyo's underworld via subway entrances.

In need of some refreshment, I wander into a 'Lawsons' convenience store. I linger a while, savouring the cool, conditioned air and shelves of unfamiliar food, before opting for some 'Black Black' caffeinated chewing gum (which according to the packet is 'Hi-technical, Excellent Taste and Flavor') and a bottle of what looks like green tea. Drifting back out into the heat, I find a shady bench and sit to watch the thousands upon thousands of black-haired blood cells, flowing through the veins of this mega-city.

I seem to have found a place popular with young fashionistas. Tokyo youths mill around, chatting, laughing and taking pictures of one another. Within minutes, two giggling teenage girls have clocked me and are approaching. I continue sipping on what I have confirmed to be green tea and chewing my gum. After much conferring between themselves, one steps forward and says something in Japanese.

I smile shyly and shrug. In addition to feeling awkward because I don't understand, I'm also worried that my Black Black gum might be some type of joke sweet that has turned my mouth and lips black-black. They confer some more then try again, pulling out a mobile phone attached to a mass of dangling trinkets.

'You fon namba?'

I turn red. They giggle some more. I thought the Japanese were supposed to be shy? Not these two. Although I am semi-flattered to be getting chatted up by teenagers, I'm thankful that I don't yet have a phone number to give.

***

Back in the hotel, for three days we attended numerous talks and workshops designed to help us cope with the alien nation we had landed in. I met people from all over the English-speaking world and many outside it: Americans, Canadians, Australians, New Zealanders, South Africans, Irish, Jamaicans, Finns, even a Luxembourger. Friendships were formed, email addresses exchanged and visits promised. But after three days of drunken, jetlagged immersion into this brave new world, bus load by bus load we were whisked away to the far corners of the Japanese archipelago – corners that would become our homes for one, two, even three years – probably never to meet again.

And now the party is over. The eight-hour bus ride from Tokyo has taken me far from the metropolis, over the Japanese Alps and to a secluded region that even the average Japanese person could tell you very little about.

After a week surrounded by hundreds of other excited English speakers all bursting with the 'first-time-in-Japan' high, I'm now sitting alone in my new apartment with no phone, no friends and almost no Japanese speaking ability.

This is when I realised things might be a little tougher than I had thought.

***

Luckily for me, school is out for the summer and I have a month off to get settled. My new home is a one-bedroom apartment in an ugly, three-storey block on a quiet back street. It has a lounge, separated from the kitchen by sliding, papered partitions; a small wash-basin in the hall; a shower room with a deep Japanese-style bath and a separate squatter toilet (with no fancy electronics) that has been converted for Western bottoms with a special seat attachment.

In place of carpets, there are rice-straw mats called *tatami* in the bedroom and lounge, which smell of wet hay. For Japan, the apartment is a generous size and ample for one person. It's furnished with a toaster oven, fridge and rice-cooker but there is no air conditioning, no central heating, no hot-water source other than the shower, and no bed; I will spend the next two years sleeping on the floor.

I survey the land from my narrow balcony. Through the sweltering haze I see a white, wooden castle, forested mountains and pea-green paddies. Lots of paddies. In fact, the name of what was my new home town, Ono, translates as 'big field', a pretty accurate description. The thick, muggy air is pulsating with the cicada's song and legions of little frogs chirp from the paddy pools. I look out over the lush, sub-tropical landscape and wonder how snow could ever fall from Ono's sticky sky.

Back in my lounge, I sit in the jet stream of a lint-encrusted fan, the only source of cooling I have. I'm not accustomed to the claustrophobic heat and humidity which makes me sluggish and drowsy. A droplet of sweat rolls from the tip of my nose and plummets to the *tatami* mat upon which I sit. My eye catches a movement. Tiny creatures are crawling in between the *tatami* fibres. Dread washes over me as I realise what they are: *dani*, blood-sucking dust mites that make their homes inside these mats.

Why did I come here? What have I got myself into? I start to wonder what other creepy-crawlies might be lurking in my apartment. Wolf spiders? King-sized hornets? The much feared *mucade* – a repulsive venomous centipede? The fact that I have inherited from the previous tenant an anti-insect arsenal capable of wiping out half of

Japan's arthropods suggests that I will be sharing my apartment with many unwelcome roommates.

I grab a can of insecticide from the selection of chemical weapons and begin to gingerly inspect the nooks and crannies of my new abode, trigger-finger poised to blast any intruders with a jet of toxic spray.

***

The following day, I set out to explore the narrow streets of my new neighbourhood on foot. I discovered a shallow river confined by concrete banks, a handful of small shops and plenty more rice paddies, but I quickly wanted to go further afield and decided I needed a bike.

Bikes seemed to be a popular form of transport in Japan and already I had seen students and OAPs alike riding the ubiquitous *mama-chari* 'granny bikes' everywhere.

When I say everywhere, I mean it. They ride their bikes on the left side of the road (the right way), on the right side of the road (the wrong way) and on the pavement. Equipped with a large basket, a low cross bar but no gears, *mama-chari* are all about affordability, practicality and functionality rather than fashion, and almost everyone in Japan seems to have one.

I had to walk for almost an hour under the heavy sun to reach Mitsua, the giant supermarket on the outskirts of town that sold everything from *wasabi* (horseradish) flavoured peas to *pot-to* (hot water bottles) to buy my bike, but it was worth the journey. It was here in Mitsua that I had my first taste of the kindness of strangers, something I would continue to experience throughout my stay and one of the reasons why I came to feel so at home in Ono.

Stepping out of the horrific heat into the air-conditioned supermarket I feel instant bliss. I pause to bathe in this deliciously cool air, but am immediately startled by the cashier girl who shouts something loudly at me. Her call of *'irashaimaseeeeee!'* (welcome!) is repeated by the next cashier, and the next, and the next. Like a verbal

Mexican wave it travels around the store, eventually petering out somewhere in the distant aisles of the giant building. I bow my head awkwardly, not knowing if a response is expected or not, and scuttle off to begin browsing this amazing world of exciting new products.

For the newly landed foreigner in Japan, even the humble supermarket is a tourist attraction. Everyday Japanese commodities present a new landscape of items to decipher: refreshing isotonic drinks with unrefreshing names like 'Pocari Sweat' and 'Calpis', creatures of the deep that I'd never before seen, parts of animals I never knew you could eat, whole aisles of alien vegetables and jars of pickled oddities.

Feeling hungry, I pop a box of sushi (one of the few items that is vaguely familiar) into my trolley and continue browsing when I feel a presence behind me. I turn slowly to find that I'm being followed. My stalker is an old Japanese man, wearing a gnarled baseball cap. I pick up the pace but he matches my speed. What does he want? Is hunting *gaijin* (foreigners) still a legal sport here?

I decide the best course of action is to shake him. Fast. I lure him into the women's underwear section. But the selection of petite bras and knickers don't distract him at all – he's still on my tail and his trolley skills are strong. I hook a left into 'Insect Zone', hoping the plastic tanks of live rhinoceros beetles will provide the diversion I need to make my getaway. But no, he's still following. What was I thinking? Insect Zone is no place for an old man; beetles are for kids. How am I going to escape? I'm running out of options.

I have no idea what I've done to attract the attention of the old timer who is now homing in on me like a *gaijin*-seeking missile and I don't really want to find out either. I have one last trick up my sleeve: the alcohol aisle. Surely no Japanese male will be able to resist the temptation of Asahi Super Dry, Sapporo Black Label, or the Nikka Whisky sold in three-litre plastic bottles? I have to try. It's the only hope I have of making a clean exit.

I glance behind; I can't see him. I think it's worked, freedom is close. Just a little further and I'll be at the checkout. Keep going, don't look back. But just as I think I'm in the safe zone, the old man steps out in front of me, blocking my path.

This time there is no escape; with his superior knowledge of Japanese supermarket layouts, he's taken a short cut through the dog food aisle and intercepted me.

The man says something in Japanese that I don't comprehend and beckons me to follow him. 'I've only been here a few days and I've already pissed the locals off' I think to myself. Assuming I've made some sort of horrific cultural faux-pas, I reluctantly follow him all the way back to the fish section, wondering and worrying what I've done to deserve this. He points to a box of sushi on the shelf. It's identical to the one in my basket; I look at him blankly.

The old man can see that I'm puzzled. Why would I want to swap my box of sushi for one that's exactly the same? So he plucks the box from my basket and makes the switch himself, carefully pointing out the price sticker on each. Suddenly I understand why we've been running up and down the aisles for the last five minutes like a Japanese 'Benny Hill' sketch. As with supermarkets back home, fresh produce is reduced in price at the end of the day. This old man, whom I had never met before, had noticed that my box of sushi was still full price, and had gone to the trouble of chasing me half way around the supermarket to bring this to my attention. I give him my best bow and a big *domo arigatou gozaimashita* (thank you very much). He smiles, says *iie*! (it's nothing!), bows back and disappears off into the fishing tackle section. I never saw him again.

***

Geared up with my bike I could now begin to explore more of the town that I would call home for the next two years. I say town, but in fact my new home, with a population of 37,000, was officially classed as a *shi* – a city. All over rural Japan, numerous municipal mergers have created what are officially cities, but are actually just a collection of small towns, villages and hamlets going under one name. This meant Ono lacked one vital criterion that all other cities I have ever visited possess: large volumes of people. By Japanese standards, Ono (and indeed the entire prefecture of Fukui) was considered *inaka* – a rural backwater. There was little traffic and few people around. Where was everybody hiding? Ono was the only 'city' I've ever been to that had no rush hour, no hustle and no bustle.

In those first few days, I spent my hours pedalling along the quiet roads of the town. Although completely encircled by a 360-degree ring of mountains, Ono itself was a plateau; the only way in or out was either over the peaks, or through the tunnels. This made it ideal for cycling; the narrow roads that ran through the paddies were quiet and the land was flat. But I did soon discover that there were serious hazards at large for the cyclist in Ono: the *gaijin* traps.

Throughout Japan and especially in rural areas, there are drainage networks consisting of channels, streams and ditches, built to cope with the heavy rain and snow. What makes them so dangerous to the unwary is that every few dozen metres a panel covering the channel will be missing without warning or reason. You could be happily walking or cycling along the side of a road only to plunge suddenly into a pungent abyss.

They seem such an obvious hazard, it's hard to believe that the country which gave us Nintendo, the Bullet Train and heated toilet seats would allow them to exist; therefore it's foreigners who are their biggest casualties.

During my stay these traps would injure *gaijin* legs, eat *gaijin* bicycles and even claim a couple of *gaijin* cars.

***

Two weeks had now passed since my arrival in Ono and having explored my local neighbourhood, it was time to go further afield. One morning after peeling myself from the *futon*, showering away the night's perspiration, and plugging a one hundred yen coin into the vending machine outside my apartment to release a can of cold coffee, I jumped on my bike and pedalled off towards the outer fringes of the town.

The distant mountains were already beginning to warp with the rising heat of the morning as I passed a nearby school. The baseball team trooped past in pairs, chanting '*Ichi! Ni! San! Shi!* (One! Two! Three! Four!). Further on, a stooped old woman, back bent like an angle-bracket from a lifetime of toil in the paddies, stopped and stared, mouth agape, as I cruised by. She wore a large brimmed bonnet and white gloves to protect her skin from the strong August sun.

I pedalled on, down through Ono's temple town, a narrow street lined with beautiful traditional temples but blighted by concrete constructions too. I reached Ono's natural spring, where cool water bubbled from the ground filling a shallow pool. An old man was crouched at the well-side. Using the ladle he scooped a cupful of water into his hands and drank.

This source of water is also a source of pride; one of Ono's proudest claims is that it has the 'third purest water in Japan'. It also boasts the 'number one brightest night sky' and 'easiest-to-see stars' in the country. Japan is obsessed with such rankings and almost everywhere has devised something for which they can rank themselves as a 'Top 10' town.

I pedalled onward towards the mountain outline when suddenly I had a sense that something was different about today. You see, I had just ridden past a group of ten people – together at the same time. Until that moment, I had never seen more than five people in one place at one time in Ono, so I knew that something really big must be going down today. I pulled a 180 on the bike and was soon hot on the heels of the local Ono-ites, sniffing out the action.

My inquisitiveness was rewarded. I had stumbled upon the biggest gathering of people I had yet seen in Ono. It seemed that all of the town's inhabitants had come out of hiding to attend an annual market that drew traders from miles around to sell arts, crafts and all manner of food produce.

There was *nihonshu* (rice wine), *shochu* (a spirit made from barley, potatoes or rice) and beer; unidentifiable vegetables; soil-encrusted roots and baskets of mushrooms; bags of small, dried fish; bamboo toys and crates of Fukui's most famous export: Echizen spider crab.

It occurred to me that perhaps the residents of Ono ventured from their lairs for this one weekend to purchase provisions for the hibernation period, which then lasts until the market returns the following year.

Being the only foreigner around, I was subject to a good deal of goggle-eyed looks and stares. They had no qualms about gawking at me and unsubtly nudging their friends to spread the word of the foreigner sighting. I was amused that they were so bemused to see a foreigner and I enjoyed the attention (though in later months my feelings on this matter were to change).

Once the initial shock of seeing a non-Japanese person in Japan had passed, the locals were keen to chat and offer me their wares. A bald, smiley man with thick, black glasses gave me a slice of giant octopus tentacle; a pretty girl with a red headscarf handed me a sample of wine from Ono's very own vineyard; and one old woman tried (but failed) to tempt me with an entire squid-on-a-stick that was sizzling away on her makeshift barbecue, filling the air with a fishy pong.

By this time, I had learnt some basic Japanese phrases, enough to explain to the inquisitive locals that I was an *Eigo no sensei* (English teacher), that I was *Igirisu kara kimashata* (from England) and that I was *niju-go sai* (twenty five years old). They all agreed that this was *ii desu yo* (good) and even went as far as congratulating me on my Japanese-speaking ability.

It was nice of them to say so, but I later came to realise that this is more courtesy than complimentary. Utter a simple '*konichiwa!*' (good day!) to a Japanese person and it's easy to trigger the '*Nihongo jouzu!*'

(your Japanese is excellent!) response, even if your *Nihongo* is not *jouzu* in the slightest.

It was at this market that my taste buds fell in love with something new: *takoyaki* (fried octopus balls). These are not the testicles of an octopus. They are small cubes of octopus tentacle encased in a ball of batter and fried, served with a delicious barbecue-style sauce on top. *Takoyaki* are fast food, often sold from street-side stalls to be eaten on the go, and are akin to a post-night-out kebab in the UK.

As the market wound down for the day and the traders began to pack up, I headed home, satisfied that I had been part of something special and loaded with purchases including a miniature bamboo bow and a box of six more *takoyaki*. It had been an excellent day and nice to finally meet more of the locals and try out some Japanese, but I wondered if I would ever again see a gathering of such magnitude in the city that always seemed to be sleeping.

***

I had already learned that there were a handful of fellow foreigners living in the area but most had chosen to escape Japan's heavy summer. After several days with no one to talk to, I was desperate for some English-speaking interaction. Luckily for me, somewhere on the coast of Fukui, a small Japanese reggae music festival was taking place and I had been invited to join a group of other newcomers on the beach for some very welcome conversation.

It was already dark as we supped on cans of *chu-hi*, a fruit-flavoured alcopop and warmed ourselves by a driftwood fire. The waves washed over the fine sand as we looked out over the Sea of Japan, spying the occasional twinkle of a fishing boat or perhaps a freighter returning from South Korea. Baggy basslines wafted over the airwaves as we spoke of our home countries and shared all the exciting new things we had discovered so far. We watched the dancing flames lick the night air and stared deep into the orange embers. As often happens when young people gather in the company of alcohol and the vicinity of water, it wasn't long before the idea of a swim was raised and we were stripping off and dashing into the ocean for a late night dip.

Due to swarms of jellyfish that appear in coastal waters at certain times of the year, Japan has an official swimming season, the dates of which are fixed and bear no relation to whether the jellyfish have actually appeared or not. The day the closed season begins, no Japanese person will enter the water. The swimming season had ended just a few days previously, but us foreigners, being foreign and all, didn't feel the need to adhere to such minor details, presuming there must be a few days leeway with the timings. After all, who was telling the jellyfish it was time to turn up? Did they check their diaries and set their Sat Navs for Japan's beaches in order to arrive precisely at the end of the swimming season? Of course they didn't. Jellyfish just drifted on the ocean currents, pulsing their way around the seas, never choosing where to go, nor when to stop.

We ran down the beach at full pelt and dived into the cool, salty water. It was a refreshing escape from the balmy night air and the *chu-hi* was enhancing the experience perfectly. I swam slowly on the calm surface for a spell as gentle waves rolled in, then dived down into the inky depths and reached for the rippled bed. But I dove too deep.

Something brushed against my leg. Then I felt a sudden, fiery jolt zap my back. Then my arm. Then my neck. Tentacles were reaching out in the darkness, injecting me with microscopic portions of poison. I rushed to the surface, galloped out of the shallows and back up the beach, frantically brushing at my burning skin.

Back in the glow of the fire, I nursed my impressive wounds as others gathered round to see. My body looked as though it had been lashed with a bull whip; angry, tentacle-shaped lines marked my skin. Thankfully it looked worse than it felt. The pain was not intense but it was several hours before the fiery sensation began to fade, and the red weals remained for days.

I conceded that Japanese jellyfish were actually quite advanced and that they did have diaries and Sat Nav after all. I promised to pay closer attention to Japan's official seasons in future.

***

The jellyfish incident was a painful spike in an already steep learning curve. Despite Fukui's, slow, rural nature, I was constantly being bombarded with enormous amounts of data about my new environment: new words, new places, new foods, new faces. Every day was an adventure into the unknown, a hugely stimulating but sometimes overwhelming experience. I had 'signed up' for Japan, ready and willing to learn, but no one had told me that soothing jellyfish stings or dodging the sewerage system would be on the curriculum.

My summer holiday honeymoon was drawing to an end. Soon it would be my turn to become the teacher as the start of the school term loomed closer although it was already obvious that as a foreigner in Japan, I would never stop being a pupil. And before classes began, I had a mountain to climb.

Chapter 2
Journey to Fujisan

You can tell how high you are on Mount Fuji, not just by the degree of altitude sickness, but by the price of the drinks. On the lower slopes, a bottle of green tea from a vending machine costs 200 Yen. By the time you've reached the mountain's barren summit, the price has tripled.

Fuji's gently sloping, almost perfectly symmetrical volcanic cone is a potent symbol of Japan and climbing all 3776 metres of it is something that most Japanese people attempt once in their lives.

A dormant volcano since 1708 but still classed as active, the threat of eruption doesn't dissuade the 300,000 people who climb it each year. Though reaching the summit requires no special mountaineering expertise, it's certainly no walk in the park. Mention Mount Fuji to anyone who knows anything about it, and it won't be long before the 'ancient Japanese saying' is regurgitated:

'A wise man climbs Fujisan once, a fool climbs it twice.'

Indeed, most accounts of climbing Fuji I had read described a gruelling hike, horrific queues, altitude sickness, biting icy winds, a death risk from falling rocks and extortionate prices. None of the foreign Fukui old hands seemed to have anything good to say about the experience and I began to wonder if perhaps the ancient saying should be modified to:

'A wise man doesn't bother to climb Fujisan. He just admires it from the bullet train.'

A few weeks after my arrival in Japan, the chance came to join the annual Fuji trip. It would likely be the only opportunity I'd get; the official Fuji climbing season lasts just two months, from the 1st of July to the end of August. Outside of this period, the mountain huts are closed and the weather conditions make the climb far more hazardous. Following the jellyfish incident, I had no intention of ignoring any more of Japan's official seasons and despite the less than enthusiastic reports of the Fuji experience, I signed up straight away.

***

After an eight-hour bus drive from Fukui City, our climbing party arrived at base station five, the starting point of the most popular climbing route. Here, a gaggle of shops were selling woolly hats, Fuji postcards, rice snacks, energy bars, tacky trinkets and even portable canisters of oxygen.

I was fairly sure that lack of oxygen would not be a problem, and scoffed slightly at one Japanese man who was buying so many canisters he seemed to be under the impression that the peak of Fuji was so high it reached the vacuum of outer space.

I did however purchase a stout wooden hiking stick to help me on my way. The stick came adorned with two bear bells and a small Japanese flag.

We had timed our journey from Fukui to arrive at this base station by late evening. Witnessing sunrise on Fuji is the 'must see' aspect of the climb and by setting off in the dark and hiking through the night, we planned to reach the summit just before the sun peeped over the horizon. Everyone was in high spirits, full of excitement, pumped up and raring to take on Japan's highest mountain. By 10pm, hiking boots were laced up, backpacks were shouldered and we began to move out.

Fuji's shadowy outline loomed above as our mass of foreign bodies merged with groups of Japanese climbers. It quickly became difficult to see who was who in the darkness, and within ten minutes, I had been swept along by the torrent of Japanese hiking parties and lost my own climbing team. I walked on, continually looking back to see if I could locate my friends but all I could make out were streams of brightly clad Japanese.

I resigned myself to the fact that it would be a lonely climb. I continued onwards alone (as alone as one could be with dozens of fellow Japanese hikers), passing though pine and birch trees, which quickly thinned, giving way to stunted scrub then bare rock. My bear bells jingled annoyingly as I walked; my Japanese flag hung limp. Then, looking ahead, I caught sight of two young ladies I recognised from the bus. Realising it would be my only chance for some English-speaking company, I powered onwards to catch them.

Sarah and Kim, two athletic Americans, were also new Fukui arrivals. Had they been here 137 years earlier, they would have been climbing illegally. It wasn't until 1868 that the government ban prohibiting women from climbing Fuji was lifted, after Englishwoman Lady Fanny Parkes boldly defied the law and trekked to the summit.

'We're training for a half-marathon.' Sarah explained.

'This is our warm-up.' Kim added.

Anyone who regards climbing Mount Fuji as a mere 'warm-up' is obviously in pretty good shape. I had planned to take it easy, but my idea of a leisurely cruise had just vanished. I was now involved in a mountaineering mission. Sarah and Kim were going for a record-breaking climb time and it looked like I was going with them. After all, I couldn't let two girls beat me to the top, could I?

So, up we went, along the narrowing rubble trails, switchback after switchback. No talking, no time for breaks, no waiting in line. Our freshly formed trio powered up paths, scrambled up rock faces, and criss-crossed through queues of Japanese who – equipped with their 60-litre rucksacks and telescopic climbing poles – seemed content to wait. We went off road and on road; we took back paths, high paths and low paths. At times we used our hands to help us clamber up steep rocky sections or cling to rope holds, but never did we stop moving or even slow our pace.

By the time we reached the 300 Yen drink mark, the crowds had thinned and the mountain was quiet. The terrain was now bare and sterile, with little in the way of vegetation. The only visible life forms were the occasional Japanese couple resting together under blankets in the shadows. They had an annoying habit of shining their one thousand gigawatt head torch beams straight into my eyeballs and burning out my retinas.

'*Ganbatte*! (keep going)' they whispered.

'*Ganbarimasho*! (we will)' we gasped back.

Below, little snakes of glowing lights shuffled their way up the mountainside. Above, the dark cone loomed high into the night sky. The air was now cold. We had left the heat and humidity of the Honshu summer far beneath us.

We continued climbing higher and higher into Japan's troposphere. At the 400 Yen drink mark I could feel the air thinning and my breathing became shallow. My steps started to become laboured, my legs felt weighty. I was beginning to feel light-headed, as if I might just topple backwards and tumble all the way down the mountain; if only I had a can of oxygen. I wondered whether I'd be able to match Sarah and Kim's pace for much longer. Our quick ascent though the lower stages meant I had worked up quite a sweat. Now my damp T-shirt was rapidly cooling, clinging to my back in the most uncomfortable way as a cold wind began to feel us out.

Sarah and Kim were showing no signs of tiring and continued to lead the way. Not wanting to admit fatigue, I kept up with the pace, but knew I couldn't last for much longer.

A small wooden hut appeared ahead, offering warmth, refreshment and the chance of rest. My spirits lifted. A nice cup of hot, green tea and a *takoyaki* or two and I'd be ready to continue our journey. But Sarah and Kim were keen to keep moving; this was, after all, just a warm-up. So we passed on by, leaving its welcoming, cosy glow behind us. My bear bells were still jingling annoyingly and my Japanese flag was now buoyant in the wind.

We walked deeper into the night and further into Japanese airspace as clear skies revealed the glimmer of stars above. After three hours, we were sure we were making good time and guessed it could be no more than another couple of hours to the top. We continued upwards, trudging over a mixture of jagged volcanic rock, dusty earth and heavy boulders. Little was said. By the time we reached the flattish plain of the next rest hut, the probing wind had turned into a piercing gale.

We agreed it would be a good place to stop for a minute, eat a snack and put on gloves. So we donned our warm clothes, gobbled rice crackers, and tried to decipher what was yet to be climbed.

It was dark. Too dark to make out the black shape of the mountain against the black sky and the path seemed to have disappeared. The wind bit into us as we wandered about trying to relocate the trail, but it only seemed to head down. My bear bells were now jingling so annoyingly that I tore them off in a fit of rage; my Japanese flag was flapping proudly.

Where had the path gone? Had we taken a wrong turn and lost our way? Perplexed, we found a Japanese duo under a blanket, and asked in fluent Japenglish where the path to the top was. Their answer bemused us:

'*Koko desu* (here)'.

We were convinced they had misunderstood the question. This was clearly not the top of Fuji. We could see no signs that would denote such a famous landmark. Mind you, it was pretty dark. The only evidence of man was yet another *torii* (traditional Japanese gateway), a hut (which was shut) and a few vending machines (selling bottles of green tea for 600 Yen). Previous accounts suggested the climb to the top would take about five hours, so we expected at least another hour to go. But after further exploration of our surroundings, repeating the question to some other Japanese climbers and even throwing in a bit of sign language, we finally became convinced; we were standing on the very top of Japan.

I was relieved that I had managed to keep up with my super-fit female companions, but now we had an unexpected problem. Not having planned to reach the summit so early, we faced a very cold, three-hour wait, if we wanted to see the all-important sunrise. We were rapidly cooling down since we'd stopped moving and the biting icy wind was whipping over us, penetrating our clothing and stealing our precious body warmth.

We sought shelter in the only place we could find: in front of a small stone building that smelled of wee. The three of us sat tightly huddled together, shoulder to shoulder, thigh to thigh, sharing what little body heat we had left, shuddering and watching the minutes tick away ever so slowly. The only others atop the mountain were a handful of Japanese lurking in the shadows, sleeping under silver space blankets. For Kim, Sarah and me, it was a time of silent triumph, a time of bonding and a time of uncontrollable shivering, but we took pride in the fact that at that very moment, we were surely the highest American-English trio in Japan.

Thirty minutes later, more of our party peaked, and like us, had difficulty believing they were at the top. It didn't take much to get them to join the huddle and soon there were seven of us shivering. An hour later, just as core body temperatures were falling below critical levels, the small hut opened its doors and we piled in, along with dozens of other Fuji refugees, for some very welcome warmth and the best bowl of steaming *miso* soup I'd ever tasted.

By sunrise, the crowds had caught up and long queues snaked down the mountainside. As the first rays of dawn struck the summit, hundreds of hands reached for camera phones and captured the essential proof of Japan's number one 'must see' – sunrise on Fuji. Slanted columns of light punctured the clouds, revealing a sea of mountain peaks stretching into the distance and a glassy lake shimmering below. It was a beautiful scene but severe fatigue, near hypothermia and sharing the view with half the population of Tokyo did reduce the effect somewhat. I peered into Fuji's dark crater, which had last spewed the contents of Mother Earth's stomach over Tokyo in 1707. Now it was just a massive hole lined with cold, black rock.

By 5am it was light, I was freezing and Sarah was complaining of headaches and nausea; altitude sickness was kicking in. After getting my hiking stick branded just to prove I really had made it, we began the descent. As we chased the retreating night shadow down the mountain, we could finally see what we had been walking on: a Martian landscape of red and ochre earth, rock and rubble, devoid of all life, shrouded in cloud and mist. We wearily snaked down the paths of clinking volcanic cinder, longing for rest. It was hard going for legs that were already spent and many fell, but my now bell-less hiking stick served me well so I was spared that embarrassment.

Two and a half hours later, we reached base camp and collapsed to the ground, exhausted. Hundreds of other climbers milled around, some recuperating like us, many preparing for their own ascent, buying oxygen canisters and hiking sticks with annoying jingly bear bells.

The famed Fuji horses trotted about, touting for business; 300 yen to pose for a picture, 4000 to be taken half way up on horseback.

One by one, the rest of our weary climbers rolled in, covered in ash and dust. We swapped stories, ate *yakisoba* (fried noodles) with grated red ginger for breakfast and dozed in the warm morning sun.

There were a range of emotions on display: tears of joy for having returned alive from the 'merciless chunk of ash'; rage from those caught in the horrendous queues who felt they were being 'slowly and painfully driven to an icy slaughterhouse'; bitterness at having been tricked into climbing 'Goddamn Fujisan!' in the first place, and just quiet satisfaction at having conquered the beast.

Devin from Detroit came limping in with a sprained ankle and a ragged shoe that had been opened by a jagged piece of cinder. Dana from Texas had been wounded by a falling boulder the size of a football, and Emily from New Zealand had taken a wrong turn on the way down, ending up in the neighbouring prefecture and sustaining a hefty taxi fare to get back to base. Brandon, an enthusiastic American from Washington State who seemed the type normally to embrace such activities as mountain climbing was furious at having been denied the summit sunrise by the huge volumes of people:

'The sun started to rise whilst I was about 15 minutes from the top. Everyone started cheering . . . but I didn't cheer. Because I am a foreign bastard.'

By twelve noon our entire climbing party had been accounted for, safe but shattered, and we boarded the bus. The return journey was considerably more sedate than the outgoing one. Most people enjoyed a well-earned sleep after promising themselves never, ever to return to Fuji again. However, thanks to Sarah and Kim, my two new fitness-freak friends, we avoided the crowds and were able to enjoy the mountain itself.

Call me a fool, but I would even go as far to say that I might climb Fuji a second time . . . just probably not for a while.

***

Fuji was the highest mountain that I climbed, but it wasn't to be the hardest. I didn't know it then, but there were more adventures at altitude to come, thanks to the knowledge and kindness of a local mountain climbing legend, who would later lead me deep into the snowy backcountry of the Okuestu range.

However, the next challenge for me would come from people rather than peaks. The new school term was poised to start and I was about to become the new object of curiosity for 150 Japanese kids, most of whom had never before met the strange creature that is a real, live, talking, walking Englishman.

Chapter 3
Lessons in Laughter

'Samu sensei, have you ever play sex?'

This is not a question a teacher would expect to be asked by a pupil, but then fifteen-year-old Shogo Iwata was no ordinary student. Outspoken and completely without shame, he used his grounding in English to further his knowledge of foreigners in a way that no other Japanese person ever dared.

'What colour is your under hair?' was another question Shogo asked me with complete sincerity. Of course, what he meant to say was:

'What colour is your pubic hair?' but nine out of ten for effort.

'Purple.' I told him, information that was quickly relayed back to his two friends, sparking some serious discussion. I also considered schooling him in the slang form, 'pubes', but decided that was a lesson for another day.

***

It was now September and the terrible heat of the Honshu summer had begun to fade. The days still burned hot, but the heavy humidity of July and August had passed. I was hugely grateful for this respite; sleeping became easier and my shirt spent less time glued to my back. After a month of exploring my new home, it was time to start work.

At 7:30 on the morning of my first day, I climbed into my car and set off on the fifteen-minute drive. I wound through the backstreets of Ono, out along the rice roads and past rounded mountains that rose from mist-covered paddies. As I neared Shotoku Junior High, kids dressed in their sailor-like uniforms riding identical bikes were converging on the school. I parked my Suzuki Wagon and stepped out of the car. The students had already spotted me and whispered excitedly as I strode into the foyer, removed my shoes and placed them in my designated cubby hole, which had already been labelled 'Samu' in *katakana* script.

'Hello! How are you? I am fine thank you!' one boy shouted, much to the amusement of his friends, before scooting off down the corridor to spread the news: there was a new foreign face in town.

I donned my indoor-only shoes and headed towards the staff room as butterflies took flight in my stomach. Passing the giant trophy cabinet, I slid open the staff room door. One man was frantically photocopying, others were hunched over laptops; all seemed occupied. Upon spying me, a loud '*Ohayo gozaimasu*! (Good morning!)' bounced around the room. I nodded awkwardly and returned the greeting.

It was good to see a familiar face. Ida *sensei*, my supervisor whom I had already met upon my arrival to Fukui, shuffled over and led me to my new desk. The headmaster then appeared from his office and everyone stood up. He spoke for five minutes during which I understood nothing, apart from the words 'Sam *sensei*' at the very end. Teachers are normally referred to by their surname with the suffix of '*sensei*' (teacher), but for foreigners, this protocol didn't seem to apply. That was my cue to deliver my introductory speech to my new colleagues, which I had prepared with the help of a phrasebook. It was met with a few nods and murmurs of '*ahhh...so ka*' ('I see') before they all hurried off to attend their duties. Everyone seemed very busy. Suddenly I was all alone in the staff room, wondering what I should do and where I should go. It was to become a familiar scenario.

***

The thought of teaching my first class had been troubling me, so I was pleased to learn that rather than launching into lessons straight away, the first week of term would be filled with the final preparations for one of the most important events in the Japanese school calendar: sports day. All summer long, pupils and teachers had been readying themselves, toiling before school, after school, even on weekends.

Everything had to be perfect and was being rehearsed repeatedly: the opening ceremony, the speeches, the school orchestra playing the school song, even some of the races themselves!

Finally, with much excited chatter flowing through the corridors, the big day arrived. Unfortunately for Shotoku Junior High, it arrived exactly the same day as a typhoon. A typhoon is the Asian word for a hurricane: a cyclical weather pattern that gains its power over the ocean and then unleashes all of Mother Nature's fury in the form of violent gales and horizontal rain when it hits land. But everyone had put so much effort and so many hours into the preparations that they weren't going to let a massive cyclonic storm with 160-mph winds and torrential downpours spoil their day. Word was given by the headmaster: let the games begin.

The day kicked off with an opening ceremony involving an impressive display of pyrotechnics. Two pupils had accessed the roof of the school and were standing on top of the three-storey building brandishing flaming torches. They used these to light a third torch attached to a zip wire, which shot down to ground level igniting a large bowl of paraffin with a satisfying 'WOOF!'. The health and safety laws that have done their best to eliminate anything resembling fun in the UK had yet to arrive here.

Next it was time to start the events. Now, when I was at kid at school, sports day consisted of sports. We had the one hundred metre sprint, javelin, long jump and the hurdles. But Shotoku Junior High's sports day consisted not so much of sports but endurance contests, the kind you might see on a Japanese game show.

The events included the 'Spin Around a Baseball Bat, Guzzle a Bottle of Coke and Sprint 50 metres' race; the 'Blind-folded Noodle Eating' race; 'Hat Battle', where three people carrying a fourth on their shoulders try to steal each others' hats; and my personal favourite, 'Tyre Tug of War', where dozens of old lorry tyres were lined up in the centre of the pitch and two teams competed to drag as many as they could back to their safe zone. Wrestling was permitted – even encouraged.

The day had begun clear and dry but shortly after the events commenced, the weather started to deteriorate. We could all feel the storm building and the black clouds looming. The wind began to grow in power; the mercury started to fall. Everyone kept glancing up at the ominous, moody heavens; everyone could feel it brooding. Nervous glances were exchanged but nobody said anything. Rain began to fall in short, powerful bursts. The spectators ducked under the cover of the tents but for the students there was no such escape.

Strong gusts of wind started to bully the crowds. A hat was removed from the maths teacher's head. A clip board was torn from the science teacher's hand. The tents began to shake: gently at first, then more and more violently as the wind tried to suck them up and dump them in a neighbouring village. The canvas started to crack loudly as it writhed and thrashed against the poles. Orders were promptly given to dismantle one of the tents before the wind did it for us. But still the games went on, now with all the spectators, teachers and announcers cowering in the remaining tent, desperately holding on to it to prevent lift off.

Fifteen more minutes passed, by which time the rain had turned torrential. Battleship-grey clouds closed in and were jettisoning their loads. The sand-covered pitch became pocked with holes, as huge tropical drops drilled the surface. With no shelter, the kids were completely soaked. Ink from their makeshift *kanji* tattoos was now running down their legs, jet-black hair stuck smoothly to their faces. I was wondering how much longer the teachers would let this punishment continue when an almighty gust of wind wrenched the giant wooden score board from its easel and sent it tumbling across the pitch.

That was as much as Shotoku Junior High was willing to take. As furious winds tore through the school grounds, the teachers leapt into action attempting to prevent loose debris from becoming weapons of moderate destruction. In winds this strong, a clip board becomes a ninja star, the pencil a bullet.

I was all but forgotten as the panicked teachers entered into the frenzy. Then I realised this was my chance to impress my new colleagues and show them that Englishmen were good to have around in a crisis. I just had to find a way of helping the cause, and looking around I saw it: the plywood scoreboard on the ground, flinching violently, threatening to take off and cause untold damage.

With absolutely no regard for my own safety, I heroically dived onto it, pinning it down. A teacher looked over to see me lying on top of it, and motioned towards the school building, gesturing I should take it inside. This was good; my act of bravery had been witnessed and would surely be reported to the headmaster. It would likely be announced in the next school assembly; I would probably be given some sort of award. But first I had to get it to the safely of the school, which was over a hundred metres away. I grabbed hold of one edge and started to heave it across the gritty pitch.

The wind was now violently raging. As I dragged the heavy burden further, I struggled to keep hold of it. Despite its weight, it became buoyant in my hands. I began to wonder if perhaps it might be better to just leave the board where it was but seeing as this was my first typhoon, and the teacher was probably a typhoon veteran, I thought it best to listen to the experts. So I continued to drag it along and it continued to flap like the wing of a pterodactyl trying to get airborne.

I was making good ground. Just another thirty metres and I would be in the safe zone; typhoon glory would be mine. But the board was wet and my fingers were slipping. I knew that at all costs I had to hold on. I must not let go. But then a gust like a bullet train screamed through and to my absolute horror, I just could not prevent the heavy board from being stolen by the storm. Wrenched from my grasp, it hurtled end over end across the pitch then smashed into a crowd of cowering kids. But it didn't stop there. I shouted a warning at the top of my lungs, but in vain; the wind took that too. Nothing could now be heard over the gale that had been unleashed on Shotoku Junior High. The giant rectangle of sodden wood struck one poor lad in the legs, knocking him to the ground, before finally coming to rest, pinned by the wind against the chain link perimeter fence.

I felt terrible. Rather than saving the day, I had managed to increase the damage done. What would my colleagues think of me now? There would be no bravery award for the Englishman after this. But the students didn't seem to be holding a grudge. They were more concerned about avoiding other shrapnel that was coming our way: bottles, plastic fans, other bits of wood. Even the sand from the pitch was stinging our bare legs, arms and eyes – we were being shot-blasted alive! There was chaos, there was panic, there was genuine fear. But still they refused to call off the games.

The grand finale was the 'cheering competition'. Of all the day's events, this one was the most important. Every single student had a part to play and it was this final, synchronised dance performance that would determine the overall winner.

There was much waving of pom-poms (both by girls and boys), synchronised dancing and even back-flips and somersaults on the now muddy, puddled surface, whilst the storm continued its torrent and the squall blasted the students. They were bedraggled, sodden and shivering but admirably, they carried on till the bitter end.

The red team was announced the champions and finally, after a day of battling the elements, everyone could take shelter from the storm. Shotoku Junior High had faced the typhoon and finished the games.

For me, it was a lesson in the Japanese trait of *gaman* – endurance and perseverance through even the most uncomfortable situations. It was something that I would become very familiar with, and occasionally infuriated by, in the months to come.

Strangely though, this 'stiff upper lip' didn't always seem to apply. A few weeks later, another typhoon struck Fukui. It was just a normal school day, with no unusual outdoor events. All the students were sent home; it was considered too dangerous to let them remain in a solid concrete building, protected from the elements. Safer to get them outside.

***

Once the excitement of sports day had passed and everyone had recovered from their typhoon-related injuries, normal lessons resumed. As my first class approached, I grew anxious. I had no teaching experience with English students, let alone Japanese ones.

I stepped into the classroom with jangling nerves. Thirty little faces locked on to 'Samu *sensei*', the outsider from a far away land. I had already been drilled by my colleague on the accepted greeting:

'Hello!' I shouted.

'Hello!' they replied in perfect unison.

'How are you?' I asked.

'I'm fine thank you, and you?'

'I'm fine, thank you.'

Then, one by one, they introduced themselves to me. Tanaka *san*, Mastumoto *san*, Shimada *san*.

I was never going to remember all these names, but it was a nice icebreaker and I began to relax as the lesson got underway. I had prepared an introductory class about England and brought some items I'd hoped to wow the students with: enlarged photographs of my family, pets and home, plus several pieces of British 'memorabilia'. The pictures were well received; the students were particularly impressed by the size of British gardens (Japanese homes tend to have little or no garden space) and thanks to the photograph of my brother's snake, the 'guess what pet?' game went down very well.

Next, I wanted to test their knowledge of the UK in return for the 'special England prize'. I asked for a volunteer and hands shot up straight away. I picked young Imata *san* and presented him with a map of the world, which I'd brought with me from home. He had one try to locate the UK. But straight away Imata *san* was puzzled. This foreign map had all the continents in the wrong place.

Whereas Europeans place Europe in the middle of their maps, believing it is the heart of planet Earth, the Asians regard Asia as the centre of the world, thus Imata *san* was presented with an unfamiliar view of the globe. Disorientated, he landed a finger on Greenland and was sent back to his seat empty handed. After eleven more vain attempts, where Australia, Iceland, Italy, Norway and Algeria were all pointed out, the UK was eventually located, much to the joy of Sawada *san*, who became the proud owner of a two-pence coin.

To finish off the class, I opened the floor to questions, which were translated by my colleague.

'Do you know David Beckham?'

'Of course! Everyone from England does,' I answered.

'Why do you dye your hair?'

'I don't, this mousey brown is all natural.'

'How many girlfriends do you have?'

I told them four, which, judging by the unimpressed nods, seemed to be a fairly average number of girlfriends to have. I actually only had one.

As the bell went, the students bowed to me and I strode back to the staff room with a great sense of relief. My first class was over. Despite my lack of teaching experience, it had gone well enough and given me a much needed dose of confidence. It was official; I was now a *sensei*.

***

I taught at two small Junior High Schools, each with fewer than 150 pupils, so it didn't take long to get to know their quirks. There were the 'cool kids' who pushed the limits of regulation hair length and style, wore their uniforms as non-uniformly as possible and who impressed me by performing multiple backflips across the concrete car park.

There were the clever kids who were sharp in class and would practise their English on me whenever we passed in the corridor. And there were of course the solitary misfits who tended to get picked on by the others.

Of all my students, it was the aforementioned Shogo Iwata who quickly became my favourite. A smiley, sporty young man, he was even more curious than his classmates about my private life and always had a question for me, usually on the topic of girls. When I set the class the task of writing poems on any subject they wanted, I expected them to write about their friends or hobbies. Shogo took an altogether different angle:

Beautiful woman
I am always thinking of
Big a bust and plump hips
Want to get they
But maybe I cannot get.
Sad.

Simple yet deep. Whether he meant to or not, Shogo created a kind of masterpiece in six short lines.

***

A few weeks into term, I was invited to join the school outing. With much excitement, we piled on to a bus and headed off along the paddy roads to a 'bakery centre', where we could learn all about the manufacture of bread. Everybody was given a small lump of dough and instructed to fashion it into anything they pleased. Most of the boys made cars, whilst most of the girls made bread replicas of the beloved *Kitty Chan*, the world famous 'Hello Kitty' cat that has been merchandised into every product possible in Japan, from cigarette lighters to love hotels.

Shogo had other plans. Ignoring the creations of his peers, he boldly shaped his dough into a fairly accurate representation of a penis. I had to commend him; the glacé cherry on the end was a particularly nice touch. When a suspicious teacher questioned Shogo as to what the phallic object was, he picked it up and started singing, claiming it was a microphone. The sniggers from his friends betrayed his façade.

Despite Shogo's amusing behaviour, his English was good and he was a hard-working and studious pupil. This could not be said for all of my students. Before my arrival in Japan, I had entertained the misconception that the stereotypically reserved nature of the Japanese means their young make angelic students. I soon discovered otherwise. I was finding that although the students' behaviour was generally good, conduct could range from mischievous and bizarre to disrespectful and, on occasion, violent. Some of the kids relished English lessons but many had no interest in learning a language that they would never need in real life. Ono was a rural, provincial place and many of the students were destined to follow in the footsteps of their parents, becoming farmers, factory employees or tradesman. Quite understandably they saw little value in learning English. I couldn't fault them for feeling this way; my native tongue had little relevance in their world.

***

Within three weeks of teaching I had discovered my nemesis: Class 2-1. I quickly came to dread our meetings, which became the low point of my week. It was like being thrown to a shoal of little black-haired piranhas. They talked loudly amongst themselves, threw things at the teachers and each other, wandered around the classroom and generally did nothing I told them. I put up with it as best I could, trying to remain upbeat whilst wishing the minutes away. But it wasn't long before the thing I had been dreading most came to pass.

It all started when Yamamoto *san*, a tall, wiry boy with zero interest in English or authority had refused to move his desk. My female teaching partner, Ikawa *sensei*, had asked the class perfectly politely to part their desks in preparation for a test but Yamamoto refused to obey. Whilst the rest of the kids were scraping their tables over the floor, Yamamoto's remained resolutely stationary. She walked over to him and repeated the order but his desk stayed put. Ikawa then decided that if he wouldn't move it, she would. That's when things turned nasty.

Yamamoto grabbed hold of the desk preventing Ikawa from moving it and a physical struggle began. I could see the danger in the situation; neither party was able to back down. Having initiated a physical confrontation, Ikawa now had to see it through, but Yamamoto was desperate to uphold his 'bad boy' image in front of his classmates.

After some initial giggles, the class went silent. The tension became unbearable as the seriousness of the situation became apparent. I had no idea what to do. Should I back up my teaching partner by joining the desk tug of war? Should I shout at Yamamoto? I didn't have the Japanese to do it, and doubted whether an English tirade would have much effect. I was utterly unprepared so ended up just standing there, watching and feeling incredibly awkward as the desk was shunted around, with Ikawa gaining ground then losing it again to Yamamoto.

The struggle came to its climax when Yamamoto let go of the desk, only to stand up with clenched fists and square up to Ikawa. I could see the adrenaline coursing through him and feared he would strike her. But then, my normally passive and rather petite teaching partner surprised me. With ninja-like speed she rebuffed Yamamoto, span him round and pinned him against the blackboard by his lapels. Their eyes were locked and their bodies rigid. Yamamoto was trembling with rage and fear. Ikawa had gone from *sensei* to samurai and had him firmly locked in position. I was petrified that it would escalate even further in to a full-blown brawl. I was always happy to assist in typhoon-related situations but felt completely out of my depth now. But then, very slowly, Yamamoto's fists unclenched, Ikawa's grip relaxed and what I feared was going to turn into an all-out-fight, was diffused. Ikawa had won, Yamamoto had backed down, and I was just relieved that it was all over. Thankfully, situations like this were rare and this class was the exception.

***

Time was rushing by quickly, the nights lengthening as the heat of summer waned. Classes were continuing well and my Japanese skills were developing, albeit slowly. Shogo was still wondering whether I had 'played sex' or not and trying to solve the mystery of my 'under hair' colour. There were a few 'I hate Japan' moments (normally during the dreaded class 2-1) but for the most part, it was an 'I love Japan' era, where everything was fascinating and new. Yes, life in Japan was flowing along nicely.

There was just one thing that was troubling me: my colleagues. Despite being impeccably polite and always pleasant, many seemed shy in my presence. My Japanese was still rudimentary, so after I had ascertained their name, preferred hobbies and favourite fruit, the conversation tended to fizzle out.

But all that changed at the *enkai*.

Chapter 4
What Happens at the Enkai Stays at the Enkai

Teachers in Japan tend to work long hours. Amongst my colleagues a ten-hour day seemed standard but they often stretched to twelve or even longer. Whether they actually got more work done than their lazy eight-hour-a-day Western counterparts is another matter. There is immense peer pressure to be seen as one of the team and to stay late just because everyone else, even if there is no work left to do. But to compensate for these long days, they reward themselves with frequent after-work parties called *enkai*.

I had heard all sorts of stories about *enkai*: embarrassing situations involving semi-naked colleagues, drunken groping and strip bars. So it was with some apprehension that I rode my bike through the warm evening air, vigilant for *gaijin* traps, en route to my first one.

My destination was a traditional Japanese restaurant inside a beautiful, old wooden house. It had a black-tiled, curly roof and was tucked away on one of Ono's narrow side streets. From the outside, it looked like any other home in the street. I had passed the building before, never realising what lay behind its sliding doors.

'*Irashimaseeee! Dozo! Dozo!* (Welcome! Come in! Come in!)' said the grey-haired *mama-san*, as I slipped in to the house slippers and was ushered up creaking stairs to a room with a *tatami* mat floor.

Scrolls depicting mountain landscapes hung on the wood-panelled walls. Two of my colleagues were squatting by a small refrigerator drinking what looked like bottles of medicine.

'Sam *sensei*! Good evening. Please, drink this. Give you power!' said the PE teacher, handing me a small brown bottle of liquid – a *genki* drink. These unnaturally luminous yellow 'health potions' contain a potent mixture of legal stimulants, minerals and vitamins and help keep the Japanese workforce awake during their long working hours. Some even contain nicotine-like compounds, perhaps explaining their popularity.

I had already noted that everyone in Japan seemed terminally exhausted. My daily greeting: 'Hello! How are you?' that kicked off every class, was normally met with a weary: 'I'm tired. And you?'

I had never seen such a nation of sleep deprivation; no wonder *genki* drinks were a staple beverage. I had seen students asleep at their desks during class (obviously they had not been drinking enough *genki* drinks) yet teachers tended to let them lie. In fact, falling asleep in public in Japan seems to be considered a sign of a dedicated worker.

'What's wrong with Yamada *san*?' I would ask my colleague.

'He's sleeping in class because he's been studying so hard,' she would reply with a sympathetic sigh.

The fact that Yamada *san* may have been playing Nintendo all night rather than burning the midnight oil studying English was not a possibility that was remotely entertained.

By 6:30pm, everyone had arrived and we took our places on cushions at low black tables. The headmaster stood to deliver a short speech to congratulate everybody on their hard work, which was followed by a toast of '*campai!*' (cheers!). The party had begun.

I sat quietly, cross-legged at the table. The smell of rice straw and sizzling fish created an intoxicating atmosphere as the *mama-san*, an old, chirpy woman deftly served *sake*, food and beer, whilst a tangle of high-speed Japanese flew over my head. I understood little of what was being said, yet I was perfectly content to just sit back and absorb this alien atmosphere. It was delightfully exotic. I couldn't help a broad smile appear. I was in Japan! I was living in a town I'd never even heard of six months ago. I was eating food I'd never before tasted, listening to a language I barely understood. And I was loving every Japanese second of it! OK, so perhaps the beer and *sake* were enhancing my mood, but I felt a warm euphoria wash over me.

Getting very drunk with your colleagues appeared to be school policy. The *enkai* is one of the few occasions when everyone can talk freely without the restrictions and hierarchy of the workplace. One way to ensure this drunken state is achieved is by never letting anyone's glass get empty. However, in Japanese drinking etiquette, it is bad form to fill your own glass; large bottles of beer and *sake* are placed on the table and it is your duty to ensure that your neighbours' glasses are always kept full.

This responsibility was taken very seriously by my colleagues. I raised my glass to my mouth and took a tiny sip of warm *sake*, reducing the volume of liquid by approximately one cubic centimetre. I lowered the glass, but before it had even touched the table, my neighbour was ready with the bottle, poised to top my glass back up to the brim. With this method of drinking, it was impossible to gauge how much we had drunk. The intensity of tomorrow's hangover would be the only measure.

Rather than each ordering a single dish, a flow of small plates to be shared were served. It was a very social banquet, far more interactive than the more solitary British way of eating. Some of the food was delicious, some less so. There was deep fried crayfish – antenna, shell and tail – all crunched up and swallowed. There was the egg sac and insides of the renowned Echizen spider crab, Fukui's most famous food. And there were all manner of sushi and *sashimi* (sliced raw fish) platters, cow intestines, pig intestines, boiled fish heads, deep-fried loach fish and a spectrum of unfamiliar mushrooms and vegetables.

As we ate deeper into the night, it became apparent that my co-workers could speak more English than they had previously let on. Though alcohol is classed as a depressant, it seems to stimulate the linguistical lobes of the brain and aid communication. With inhibitions lowered there was no fear of making mistakes. They tried out their English; I did my best to reply in Japanese. I was seeing a new side to some of my colleagues who at work seemed unfriendly or unconcerned with me. It appeared that this behaviour had more to do with shyness than lack of intrigue. Indeed, they were interested to know my opinions on Japan, as well as more personal matters.

'Sam *sensei*, what do you think about Japan?'
'Do you like Japanese food?'
'Do you have girlfriend?'
'Is she Japanese?'
'Does she live in Japan?'
'Are you married?'
'When are you getting married?'

My answers would be relayed down the table to others, eager to hear my views.

My colleagues also displayed a generosity I had not witnessed during working hours. As the *sake* penetrated deeper, offers of hospitality started to surface. The headmaster invited me on a fishing trip. The maths teacher invited me to go wakeboarding with him. The science teacher thought that perhaps we could go skiing together when winter arrived. They were opening up and sharing what they could with me. Finally, I was connecting with my workmates; I was so grateful for their kind offers and was to take some of them up later.

After two hours of continuous feasting and drinking, the so called 'first party' was drawing to a close and it was time to move on. The headmaster stood up, gave another short speech and then the *banzai*! toast. This is the equivalent to a 'hip hip hooray!' and is accompanied by much waving of hands in the air. Some months later, I was given the honour of leading the *banzai* toast. I drunkenly announced in my finest Japanese that I loved Japan, I loved Fukui and that the people of Ono were the best in the whole country. My rousing speech was met with nods of agreement and cheers.

After the *banzai*, the troops were rallied for round two of the party. Following such a huge feast, I was surprised to learn that rather than going to a bar, we were going to another restaurant for more eating! Tonight this would be a local sushi bar, but forget the modern conveyor belts of Yo! Sushi fame, this was a tiny, traditional venue.

Here, an old sushi samurai, wearing a bandana, sliced and diced great hunks of tuna, octopus and squid, and served us green tea and the finest local *nihonshu* (rice wine).

Though sushi is now an international food that can be found even on the supermarket shelves of Britain, we tend to get a sanitised version instead of the *ikura* (salmon eggs) *unagi* (eel) or *uni* (sea urchin gonads) that are popular in Japan. Indeed, I have seen boxes of 'sushi' in British supermarkets assuring customers that they contain 'No Raw Fish'! I was amazed at the amount of food my colleagues consumed that evening, and I later went to *enkai* where we ate at three restaurants in a row.

Sat on the raised wooden platform of this delightfully rustic sushi bar, I fell into conversation with the school handyman. His job was to prune the trees, rake the gravel and generally keep the school in good order. He was tall with wiry muscles and slightly unkempt hair, dyed a shade of shiny brown. We clicked straight away over our mutual love of snow, and I found his open, brasher personality an intriguing contrast to the more reserved nature of my other colleagues.

I discovered he was a keen skier and had even competed at national level, spending several winters in Hokkaido and Nagano racing and working as a ski patroller. During the summer, he had worked in the forests as a lumberjack, harvesting cedar and pine.

'If you could ski anywhere in the world, where would you go?' I asked.

'I only go to Japan.'

'But if you could go anywhere – Canada, New Zealand, France, Chile – where would you go?'

'I don't go to foreign country.'

'Why not?'

'Japan is number one!'

Handyman was also a self-proclaimed 'playboy'. He openly explained, in front of everyone, that he liked to 'play sex' with girls, and that he would sometimes go to Osaka especially to do so, because Osaka was the 'best place to play sex'.

'But what about your girlfriend?' I asked.

'Professional – no problem,' he said, claiming that his girlfriend apparently had no issue with him sleeping with prostitutes.

'But not professional – girlfriend don't like.'

To complete the evening, we moved on to a karaoke bar. This was the moment I had been dreading. I hate karaoke. Listening to poor renditions of 'I Will Survive' is not my idea of fun, and having no singing talent of my own means that embarrassing myself in front of a pub load of people has zero appeal.

Knowing I would have to do karaoke in Japan was one of the things I had least been looking forward to. However, I quickly discovered that karaoke in its country of invention was quite different to the 'Disco Dean's Karaoke Night'-style karaoke that has become popular in the UK. In Japan they do it properly. You rent a private booth, complete with disco lights, a huge TV screen, comfy sofas, and a hot line to the bar. You even get a score at the end of your song.

'Sam *san*, you like Beatles?' said the deputy head.

Being from England, it was obvious to my colleagues that I must be a huge fan.

'Erm, yes, they are good.'

'Yes Sam *san*. Very, very good. I like Beatles very much also. Please sing for us Beatles.'

He programmed several of the Fab Four's tracks into the machine and handed me the microphone. I had no choice but to try and uphold their belief that everyone from the UK was a devoted Beatles fan and knew the entire back catalogue off by heart. It sounded pretty awful, but my colleagues seemed to enjoy it, clapping along and even joining in the choruses.

By the early hours, vocal chords were failing and ears protesting. Many songs had been sung, mostly badly, and the night was coming to a close. The Deputy Head, who had taken me under his wing over the course of the evening, called for a taxi. And to make doubly sure I would get home, he jumped in the taxi too, barking directions at the driver. Five minutes later, we arrived at my apartment. He stumbled out of the car, refused my contribution to the fare, accompanied me to my front door, and then, satisfied I had been deposited safely, turned, tripped in his stupor, and fell down the stairs. He managed to get up, dusted himself off, wished me good night, and hopped into the taxi. He was much drunker than I, and it should have really been me who accompanied him home. But of course, that would never do. I thanked him for his kindness and bade him goodnight.

I loved my *enkai* experience. It had been a chance to explore obscure Japanese cuisine, bond with my co-workers and practise Japanese in an environment where it didn't matter if I got it wrong. There was just one problem. Despite all the chat, all the invites and all the fun, the following morning, relations seemed to revert back to the rigid, formal nature of the Japanese workplace.

I had expected to come in to work the next morning to join the 'Yes we're hung over, but we're all hung over together!' club, and to enjoy laughs about last night with my newfound friends. Instead, it was simply business as usual. No knowing smiles. No 'How are *you* feeling this morning?' with the implied notion that *you* had drunk Honshu's entire supply of *sake* the previous evening. I was disappointed at first, but I came to learn it was just the way it was. No matter what drunken craziness had occurred, *enkai* antics were never, ever, spoken of again.

Shortly before getting into that taxi last night, I had popped to the toilet. I returned to the table to find the Deputy Head slumped on the floor, his glasses lying on the *tatami* mat and next to a spatter of his own blood.

I'd love to tell you the whole story but what happens at the *enkai* stays at the *enkai*.

Chapter 5
Teeth Wisdom

I've already told you about the letter that arrived from the Japanese Embassy whilst I was still living in England and working at the lab. It was a big, brown, heavy letter that contained the offer of a new adventure, a new life in Japan. But I didn't tell you about the other letter that arrived that day. Small and wafer thin, it was addressed to my girlfriend.

Dear Miss Tonley,
We regret to inform you...

The single A4 sheet terminated our dreams of teaching in Japan together. It was a very sad day. I had been accepted; escape and excitement in a foreign land awaited. She had been rejected; uncertainty and insecurity lay ahead.

There were tears of course. I tried to comfort her whilst she cried and questioned herself. Even now, it makes me sad when I think of her clutching those two letters, knowing before we'd even opened them what it meant for her, for me, for us.

But one of the reasons why I love her is that she doesn't give up so easily. After several days of sorrow, we commenced work on Plan B. I would take the job and leave for Japan, she would follow a few weeks later. We'd work something out.

So, after seven weeks of early morning phone calls and lengthy emails, we were reunited. We weren't entirely sure how things would pan out, but with my new connections and her enthusiasm, we hoped things would somehow fall into place. For now, she would live with me, sleep on my *futon*, lounge on my *tatami*, borrow my car. I would adopt the traditional role of the male, gathering yen and hunting for food in the supermarket. I would provide everything she needed, for as long as she needed it. But shortly after her arrival, the day came when I was to rue our arrangement.

***

I wake in the small hours of night, in pain. A gnawing, grinding pain, deep in my jaw bone. I slink from my *futon*, over to the mirror. My reflection reveals a bulbous, inflamed gum around my lower right wisdom tooth. I swallow a couple of paracetemol and try to get back to sleep, but the painkillers aren't killing it so I have no choice but to lie awake until morning.

I reluctantly head to work, hoping it will get better. But all day it gets worse; by noon I can barely open my mouth. It takes me thrice as long to eat my lunch as I gingerly chopstick rubbery squid into the good side, and jar with pain every time it strays onto the bad side. My chewing power had been reduced to that of a baby frog's.

School finished unexpectedly early that day. Normally this would be a blessing, but on that occasion, my girlfriend had taken my car to go shopping in Fukui city. It was either wait for three hours, or walk. So I shouldered my laptop bag and began the hour-long march back into town.

Down the lane, over the little railway line and past the rusty old vending machine that once sold batteries I went. Alongside the rice paddies, under the hot sun. The pain gnawed away deep in my jaw and I cursed every step.

The kids rode past on their bikes, pinging their bells at me and calling:

'Samu *sensei*! Samu *sensei*! Bye bye Samu *sensei*!'

But I didn't want to be on show right now. I didn't want to be the smiley 'Samu *sensei*' that I always tried to be. All I wanted to do was curl up in a pain-free ball and sleep.

I nodded and strode on. Hazy layers of mountains faded into the distance, each layer fainter than the one in front. Wisps of low cloud rested halfway up the forested peaks. I reached the Kuzuryu River and traipsed over the bridge. Its shallow, stony waters flowed by concrete banks.

I passed a little wooden shrine with a row of miniature Buddha statues inside. A farmer was harvesting his rice, sat atop a tiny contraption that looked like a 'My First Combine' plaything. Feeding the golden ears into its metal mandibles, it left a trail of stubble in its wake. Large kites circled above swooping for easy pickings. Normally I would delight in such details. Not today.

I left the main road, turning onto a narrow track that ran alongside the river's flood plain. A makeshift football pitch, it was one of the very few places in Japan where I'd seen grass. Overhead power lines, draped over wooden pylons, edged the road and led the way. I plodded on, past a farmer's house where red seed spread on woven mats was drying in the sun. An old lady watched me trudge by as she hosed the hot tarmac outside her door with water. The practice is common during the Japanese summer, supposedly helping to cool the air flowing into the house.

I eventually reached the road of thin, two-storey houses and bonsai that led to my apartment block. I walked up the stairs, bothered, hot and hurting, and delved into my pocket to get my keys. Oh Fuck. My girlfriend had those too. Fuck, Fuck, FUUUCK! I was sweaty. I was tired. I had just walked for an hour under a blazing ball of Japanese fire. I was suffering from the worst pain I'd ever experienced in my entire life, and now I was locked out of my own home because my girlfriend had MY car and MY keys to MY apartment.

I was utterly pissed off. Of all the days I could have found myself carless and keyless, today was the worst possible day it could have happened. I wanted to sob; I would have done so if I'd had the energy. But instead I just collapsed in the concrete stairwell, put my head in my arms and waited, as my jaw throbbed, and a frustrated, helpless rage seethed through my arteries.

***

That night I couldn't sleep a wink. The pain was gnawing deeper and, as my girlfriend kindly informed me, my breath had begun to 'smell like rotten meat'. By the following morning there was no other option: I had to see a dentist.

For many people, visiting a dentist in their own country is not a relished experience. Visiting a dentist in another country is an even less pleasant prospect. Visiting one in Asia adds an extra point to the daunting dentist scale, and even though Japan is medically advanced with a good health care system, Japanese teeth are not renowned for their excellence.

In North America, the British have a reputation for bad teeth, but compared to some Japanese chompers, my rather average ivories were examples of excellent dental hygiene and orthodontic alignment. Braces and retainers are an uncommon sight in Japan, there is no fluoride in the water, and most brands of Japanese toothpaste only have token amounts of fluoride, if any at all.

I had already seen many Japanese mouths that had made me wince. Decaying canines, grey or brown with rot; snaggletooth incisors jutting out at unsightly angles. Many a pretty Japanese girl's face was spoiled when she broke into a smile, displaying gnashers that looked like the Predator's.

Beauty is in the eye of the beholder and straight, white teeth are not considered a necessary requirement of beauty in Japan. Some women painted their teeth black up until the Meji era, and even today, a set of crowded teeth can be regarded as attractive. It even has a name – *Yaeba* – which means 'double tooth'. It's seen as 'cute' in Japanese women and it's certainly no barrier to a modelling career. But although I was slightly uneasy about visiting a Japanese dentist, the pain wasn't going away and I needed help.

I had no idea where the dentist was, or how to get there. Fortunately, Angela, my feisty New Zealander neighbour came to the rescue, immediately calling her Japanese friend, Tomiko, to assist me.

Upon arrival in Fukui, most foreign teachers had been assigned a local Japanese family to help them in situations exactly like this. But I was an orphan; at least, I was an orphan where Japanese parents were concerned. When the people of Ono had been given the option of taking me under their wing, nobody had volunteered. So whilst my foreign friends were regularly whisked away for home-cooked meals and to be shown Fukui's famous sights, I had been left to fend alone.

Within an hour, the kindly Tomiko was at my door. A middle-aged woman with a black bob and round glasses, Tomiko had long been a friend to foreigners passing through Ono. She seemed to spend much of the year travelling the world with her husband and spoke English well. After a slightly embarrassing introduction, seeing as my breath now smelled like maggot-infested dog food, we were on our way.

The dentist was a small, two-room affair on the second floor of a narrow, white-tiled building near the centre of Ono. I waited in the tiny waiting room, clutching my jaw, whilst Tomiko explained my predicament to the masked nurse. She looked down at me with long lashes from the reception desk, nodding sympathetically.

After a short wait, I was invited into the surgery. But something had been lost in translation. This was like no dentist's I had seen before. A row of four chairs sat in front of four mirrors; three were occupied. It looked like a barbershop.

'Please. Take a seat.' beckoned the young-looking dentist, who was poking around in patient number two's mouth. I obeyed, expecting another dentist to appear, but after five minutes, no one had. Instead, the dentist, who had since moved on to patient number three, then came over to me.

'Please open,' he said, selecting a shiny instrument from his tool kit.

I opened as wide as I could, and he poked around with a metal probe, causing me to jolt in pain when he touched my inflamed gum. He then said something to the nurse and went back to patient number one.

'Japanese dentists are fast,' I thought, as I made to get up and leave, but the nurse came rushing back over and told me to stay put.

For the next ten minutes, the dentist flitted between patients one, three and four, performing a filling, a drilling or scraping a bit of plaque off here and there. Finally, this master of multitasking got back round to me, where he took another look, then sent me for an x-ray with the nurse. I returned five minutes later with my negative to await his diagnosis.

He slid the chart against the backlight, flicking a switch to illuminate my mouth, now depicted on celluloid in black and white. He murmured something and looked closer, pointing to a ghost-like, white shape at the back of my mouth. The nurse nodded in solemn agreement.

'You have advance infection of back tooth gum,' he said.

'Is it serious?' I asked.

'Infection will come again. I must extraction.' His eyes flashed with excitement at the prospect.

'Extraction? Whoa whoa . . . hold up! Let's not get carried away here!'

He then made it quite clear that he wanted to tear out the wisdom tooth that was the root of the problem, and explained that if he was going to extract one, he might as well extract all four. To make matters even worse, my x-ray had revealed a fifth wisdom tooth still buried in my jawbone; of course, that would have to go too.

I don't know if it was because it was his chance to operate on a rare breed, or just because I was a freak of dental science with my extra wisdom tooth, but he seemed very keen to carry out the operation, and spent several minutes trying to convince me.

'But this is the first time this has ever happened,' I pleaded.

'I must extraction'.

'But it might never happen again.'

He shook his head gravely.

'Extraction. Infection will come back.'

As a teenager I had been subjected to extended dental torture; there was no way anyone was tearing out all five of my wisdom teeth now, certainly not without a second opinion. So instead, I settled for some antibiotic gel which he applied with a syringe onto my inflamed gum. He then tried to interest me in the extraction one last time. To his disappointment, I declined, promising I would return if the infection didn't clear up.

I paid my small bill (the rest being covered by my employer's healthcare insurance) and left for the pharmacy with a prescription for more antibiotics, before thanking Tomiko profusely. I was relieved to be leaving with all five of my wisdom teeth still firmly attached to my jawbone.

Incidentally, the tooth trouble never did resurface. That trip was thankfully my one and only experience of the Japanese health care system – at least where I was the patient.

***

Within one month of her arrival, my girlfriend had secured a teaching job too. It came with her own apartment and car, in Sabae, a town one hour from Ono. It was ideal; now we both had our own space. I could be as messy as I liked and not start arguments and I would never be left locked out of my apartment with a sore tooth again.

Chapter 6
Animal Encounters

There was a bite in the air as I stepped out of my apartment into a cool, crisp morning. Only last week, the weather had been pleasantly warm. Now the last days of summer had passed. The mountain forests that looked down on Ono were shedding their green garb and showing off red and yellow outfits. Yes, autumn had definitely arrived and I had the scar to prove it.

I had got into a ritual of buying a can of cold coffee from the vending machine just outside my apartment block each morning. Since my arrival, I had worked my way through every single brand, finally deciding that 'Suntory Boss Rainbow Mountain Blend' was my favourite. I strolled over and posted my 100 yen coin through the slot, hitting the button for my regular choice.

'Arigatou Gozaimasu!' the machine thanked in a high-pitched female voice as the drink plunked into the tray. I bent to retrieve the can, clamped my fingers firmly around the narrow metal cylinder, immediately screamed in pain and dropped it to the ground. It was hotter than the sun. Only yesterday, this exact same brand had been ice cold. Without warning, the vending company had decided the season for drinking cold coffee was over. They had switched all their cold coffees to hot, apparently adjusting the thermostat to the 'Earth's Core' setting. I nursed my seared palm and cursed the machine; it was going to make me late for the fishing trip.

As a young lad, I had whiled away several summers on the shady banks of pools and streams in my home county of Shropshire, pulling carp, tench and trout from the water. So when the headmaster of my school kindly invited me to join him on an angling trip at my first *enkai*, I was delighted.

It turned out to be fishing alright, but not as we know it.

***

I rolled up at 8:03am at the designated meeting point, to find all three members of the angling squad already waiting. Just like their trains, the Japanese tend to be extremely punctual; when they say 8:00am, they mean 8:00am. Not 8:01am, not 8:02am and certainly not 8:03am. Feeling slightly guilty for being so late, I made my apologies, deciding to keep quiet about the coffee can incident and we were soon on our way.

Keen to ensure communication would not be a problem on the trip, the headmaster had enlisted the entire English department of the school – a grand total of two – to accompany us. I would later come to realise how scarce and precious free time was to a teacher, and that the Headmaster and Deputy Head, along with my supervisor, had all made a considerable sacrifice to take me fishing that day.

Deputy and Headmaster were men of contrasts. Headmaster was tall and dignified; he spoke slowly and quietly, always with an air of thought. He had a head of slicked-back hair and was married with two children. Deputy was small, balding, had glasses, a lazy eye and was single with no children. He tended to get very drunk at *enkai* and the staffroom rumours had it that he was addicted to *panchinko* – a Japanese gambling game which could be the love child of a pinball machine and a one-armed bandit. However, both men were very kind and welcoming towards me throughout my stay in Japan.

We set off along the paddy roads before turning towards mountains whose summits were poking through the morning mist. The way morphed from major road to minor road to narrow lane then dirt track. As the width decreased, the beauty of the scenery increased. Soon we were bumping along a slim gravel path, brushing past undergrowth that encroached from the sidelines. The path climbed, and eventually opened out at a clearing, where a small wooden hut stood. We stepped out of the car.

'Sam *san*, beautiful location,' announced Headmaster, gesturing to the lush forest, shrouded in wisps of mist.

Admiring the blue-tinted stream that was rushing down the mountainside under lolling tree branches, I had to agree.

A man in green waders and a black baseball cap appeared from the hut and welcomed us in. Words were exchanged and he shuffled off, returning a minute later with a small tub of salmon eggs – our bait.

We were soon walking up to the river to commence the hunt. A short stretch had been divided into a series of deep pools using dams of natural rock. I chose a pool, took a rod and with a salmon egg for bait, plopped my line into the stream and began the wait.

It didn't take long for the action to start. The headmaster was quick to strike and had soon pulled out a trout from the pool he was fishing in. He unhooked it, dropped it in a bucket, and cast back in.

I put his quick result down to the years of experience that he had in fishing these waters, and I continued the wait, knowing it was just a matter of time before I too was reeling in a shimmering trout.

Minutes later, he had struck again. Then again and again. After half an hour, I still hadn't even had a bite. How was my colleague managing to whip out fish after fish? He was obviously an expert fisherman, a true master of the art. He must have dedicated years to studying the habits of his quarry, in the dedicated way the Japanese do so well. I looked over, trying to discover his secret. What was he doing that I wasn't? Would all my years of childhood fishing experience count for nothing?

But my 'luck' was about to change. I heard the tuk-tuk-tuk sound of a tiny vehicle approaching. The fish man came chugging along in his three-wheeled truck, bearing a large barrel sloshing around in the back. He stepped from his cab, and with a strained grunt hefted the barrel towards me. He then proceeded to pour its contents into the pool that I was fishing in. The barrel contained water, and exactly twenty small rainbow trout.

It was at this point that I realised why 'Angler of the Year' had been having all the luck, and the terrible truth became apparent. The fish man breeds trout. You pay the fish man for a barrel of trout. The fish man pours the barrel of trout into your pool. You then proceed to catch all the trout he has just put into your pool.

I already knew that Japan had some strange ideas over what constituted fishing. I had heard of Tokyo's overstocked carp pools where *salarymen* fished in the shadow of skyscrapers. A few weeks earlier I had been bewildered to find people pulling trout from the deep end of a swimming pool at a festival in nearby Izumi village, then cooking their chlorinated catch over a poolside barbecue. But this seemed even more distant from what I considered fishing to be. It was shooting fish in a barrel, without the guns.

Now freshly stocked with a glut of trout, I began to catch fish after fish. Within seconds of my bait hitting the water, they flocked to my hook and their subsequent death. I reeled them in, dropped them in the bucket and recast my line. After twenty minutes of serial trout catching, the challenge was wearing off, but the headmaster insisted I keep going until all twenty trout had been caught. After all, he had paid for them. This may well be the first fishing story in history that doesn't need to exaggerate about 'the one that got away'. There were no 'ones that got away' that day. Every last fish was caught.

By midday we had emptied our pools of fish. We gutted, salted and skewered our haul of rather small trout (had I been fishing back home, I would have thrown them straight back), cooking them over a special fish barbecue. We then ate them Japanese style; everything apart from the head was consumed. Fins, bones and most of the spine were all crunched up and swallowed. I was reluctant at first (I tend to prefer my fish spine-free) but they were delicious.

It was an unorthodox form of fishing but I did not care. I was sitting in a mountain forest, beside a river not lined with concrete (a rare sight in Japan), munching down fresh trout with my senior colleagues. My workmates had sacrificed their precious free time, just to make me feel welcome.

Headmaster made the perfect end to the day when he announced:

'Sam *san*, they taste so much better when you've caught them yourself.'

'They sure do,' I replied with a smile.

***

If my trout could barely have been called wild, there were other animals in backwater Fukui that certainly qualified.

My arrival in Japan had coincided with some freak weather phenomena. Just days before I had arrived in Ono, a violent typhoon had caused massive flooding as several of Fukui's rivers burst their banks; 69 houses had been destroyed, 14,000 were under water, 3 people had been killed, 17 injured.

An entire railway bridge had been washed away and large sections of the line had been wrenched from their sleepers and mangled by the floodwaters. The railway from Ono to Fukui City (the prefectural capital) was no more; it would take four years to rebuild the track. But those heavy rains had another effect on the area, which was to plunge the citizens of Ono into a state of terror.

In the dense mountain forests that encircle the town of Ono, lives the Japanese Black Bear. These shy creatures are normally never seen by humans as they avoid urban areas, but the unusually wet summer had depleted much of their natural food sources and now the bears were hungry. If they couldn't find food in the forest, then they would come to the town to eat.

The Japanese Black Bear (also called the Asiatic Black Bear) is known to be one of the more aggressive species and there have been numerous incidences of them attacking and killing humans. I was surprised to learn that the Japanese hunt the bears, parts of which are still used in medicine and also eaten for meat. Bear meat is said to have a very strong, slightly unpleasant smell, which may explain why I later saw a can of bear meat in curried form (alongside a can of seal curry and a can of whale curry).

When talking to my Japanese friends about the bears, the reaction was always the same:

'I don't like bears. Bears are very dangerous Sam *san*. Very dangerous.'

There seemed to be no appreciation of these creatures as is seen in other bear countries such as Canada or the USA. Indeed, the bear threat was taken very seriously. As autumn rolled on, more and more of the large, black animals had been sighted prowling the outskirts of Ono. They were closing in on the town.

I discovered from a Japanese friend working for the council that 40 bears had already been captured, half of which had been slain. Schools were on high alert. When a bear was seen close to the grounds of Kamisho Junior High, an emergency meeting was held and the kids were immediately sent home, escorted by adults to ensure they would make it to safety before nightfall. Bear spray sales soared as the citizens of Ono readied themselves for an attack. People were afraid to go outside after dark.

Secretly, I thought the entire bear scare was being a little overplayed, and I actually quite wanted to see one (I later saw two). But when I read into it a little more deeply, even I began to fear the killer *kuma*. In 2004, there were 111 bear attacks on people in Japan, and the numbers are rising. As well as the destruction of their forest habitat, this is also due to afforestation projects that favour rapidly growing species at the expense of Japanese oak and chestnut. The trees produce food for the bears, so their loss forces the creatures out of the forests and into contact with humans in a search for sustenance.

I started arming myself with an umbrella when I walked to the Lawson *conbini* store at night. Believing its aluminium tip was an adequate anti-bear device, I kept alert as I skirted the paddies, straining my eyes for dark shapes.

It turned out the climate of fear had not been unfounded. A few evenings later, an elderly woman was found lying in the road having been attacked and mauled whilst taking out her rubbish.

She later died in hospital from her injuries.

***

Dubiously caught trout and killer black bears weren't the only animals I was encountering. When I signed up to teach English in Japan, I was told at the interview that my job would be varied.

'You should be prepared to pitch in and help out. Be flexible and do whatever is asked of you.' they said.

'Fine.' I said.

However, I never expected dog-walking to be part of my duties. As far as I knew, Kamisho Junior High was the only school in Fukui, and quite possibly all of Japan, that was lucky enough to have a school dog.

Shiro, which means 'white', was a stray. She had wandered into the school, limping badly after being hit by a car. Her owners could not be traced, so the teachers decided that she would have to be put down. However, the students had already fallen for her and when they heard of plans for the lethal injection, a mighty protest was launched. The teachers eventually gave in and Shiro was spared. She lived in a small wooden kennel at the back of the school.

I discovered that cleaning time was the best time to embark on adventures with Shiro. Schools in Japan don't employ professional cleaners. Instead, schools practice the ritual of *souji*, a time when all pupils arm themselves with cloths, brushes or brooms and set to work cleaning the school.

They were very jealous upon hearing their British counterparts didn't have to clean their schools, but I approve of *souji*, because it instils a sense of tidiness and the notion of cleaning up after yourself.

To announce the start of the cleaning period, a Japanese cover version of the disco anthem 'Y.M.C.A.' by the Village People would be played over the PA. I suspect that because of its association with *souji*, the students of Shotoku Junior High will forever hate this song, if they don't already.

The downside of having students responsible for the cleanliness of the school was their dubious quality of workmanship. Giving the impression that you're cleaning hard, whilst actually performing the minimum amount of work, seemed to be the name of the game.

The ever present smell in the toilets suggested cleaning skills could be improved.

***

It was a fine autumn day when, at precisely 2:50pm, 'Y-M-C-A!' came blaring over the PA. I left my desk and headed to the kennel. Upon seeing me appear, Shiro went berserk as normal, knowing she was in for a lengthy walk. Despite her damaged hind leg, Shiro was surprisingly strong. I clipped on her lead and she fired off like a greyhound, onto the baseball pitch and over the paddy paths, dragging me in her wake.

I had got in to the habit of buying an afternoon *genki* drink from the vending machine that sat opposite the graveyard, a short way from the school. However, today I was feeling peckish so instead, we set off towards the little village shop.

We walked along the road, over the massive red *kanji* characters painted on the surface. They warned drivers to 'give way' though it hardly seemed necessary when the most you might have to give way to was a granny on her *mama-chari* bike.

We passed a field of onions growing next to a cluster of houses, their wooden walls dark with age. Shiro, thirsty, strained to drink from the irrigation channels that rushed alongside the field. Large kites circled above, hunting creatures of the paddies.

I slid open the shop's slatted door, leaving Shiro tied up outside. The shelves were sparsely populated; a few faded boxes of biscuits, some tired looking vegetables, a packet of octopus flavoured crisps.

The wrinkled lady at the counter looked up and froze. She appeared visibly quite shocked. So shocked, in fact, that to make sure her old eyes were not playing tricks on her, asked:

'Are you a foreigner?' (she used the slightly impolite '*gaijin*' – but at least added the honorific '*san*').

I assured her that I definitely was foreign. So foreign in fact, that I was from England.

She eyed me up and down with amazement, mouth ajar. Then turned to the lady she was serving and said:

'He's a foreigner. From England.' Just in case the lady hadn't already heard the news.

She then went back to her abacus, calculating her customer's bill by flicking the coloured beads from one side to the other. Modern Japan had yet to arrive here; the old ways still ruled.

I left with a packet of 'Men's Pocky' – chocolate coated pretzel sticks – and continued our walk. The road ran on, beneath mist-shrouded mountains and past a bamboo thicket with its perfectly vertical trunks. Then alongside more paddies, rice rippling like an inland green sea as a breeze danced across the surface.

Japan is a haven for interesting animals and Shiro and I saw plenty of them. Lizards scampered from their rocky hideouts; gigantic prehistoric-sized dragonflies buzzed past hunting airborne prey; the much feared *mucade* (venomous centipede) scuttled under cover; a snake basked on black tarmac absorbing solar energy from the Japanese sun.

Yesterday I had even found a tortoise slowly plodding across the road; fearing its shell would not save it from the wheels of a Mitsubishi 4X4, I picked it up and placed it safely out of harm's way. They are not native to Japan, but the country is the leading importer of wild tortoises for the pet trade. I assume that this one was either an escapee or had been purposely released by its former owner.

Shiro took great interest in the snakes. She immediately launched an attack upon sighting one, straining on her lead to get at it. I always had an urge to release the hound and let her attack the serpent, but the thought of having to return to the kennel with the beloved school pup hanging limp in my arms after losing the fight was enough to quash my inquisitive desires, so I never did get to see the outcome of a Shiro versus snake battle. But I did get to see the outcome of a *sensei* versus snake battle.

You see, one of the hazards of rural Japan is indeed the snakes. There is at least one deadly venomous species and several that can deliver a painful bite. During the warmer months they were frequent visitors to the school.

There were several techniques for evicting these unwelcome guests from the premises, none of which caused any lasting harm. If the snake was discovered near an outer door, the large witch-like broomsticks would be used to brush it outside. This was effective with larger serpents, but sometimes smaller snakes would simply slither up into the twigs of the brush and would then be very difficult to remove.

Another method was to grasp the head of the beast with long-handled barbecue tongs and then take it, writhing violently, outside and deposit it in a paddy field. Both were effective methods of snake removal, but when a new teacher named Takada started working at the school, these methods became obsolete.

Takada *sensei* became known to me as the Snake Hunter. He had previously worked in a nature education centre and was therefore very knowledgeable about Japan's wildlife. He knew how to rid the school of snakes, not just in a safe manner, but with flair and showmanship. One day soon after he joined, a snake was spotted in school. A call went out over the PA system.

'Calling Takada *sensei*! Takada *sensei*! Snake sighted in entrance hall, please report for action!'

Within minutes, the Snake Hunter arrived on the scene, armed with his weapons: nothing more than a plastic bin liner and his bare hands. By this time, a crowd of students and teachers had gathered, eager to witness the man in action.

When a snake is threatened, it will normally retreat into a coiled position; like a wound-up spring, this allows it to quickly strike an attacker. The Snake Hunter was wise to this. His first move was to quickly tap the snake, provoking it to uncoil and extend its body. This allowed him to grasp the serpent by its tail and lift it off the ground. But whilst dangling, the snake reared up, trying to bite the hand of its captor. This was when the Snake Hunter truly asserted his authority as king of the jungle with a technique no serpent could fight. Like a caveman might swing a sling shot, the Snake Hunter swung the snake round and round his head, exerting a highly unnatural amount of G-force on its rather small brain. Rendered temporarily dazed, the hunter popped it into his plastic bag to be removed and released unharmed (though probably a little dizzy).

A true performer, the Snake Hunter nodded to the crowds of students and staff, who applauded with relief, shouting *sugoi naaa*! (amazing!) as he walked away with the bagged serpent.

The school corridors were once again a safe place to walk.

Chapter 7
A Night at Yumeya

The days of autumn were passing and the air had become sharp and clear. The cicadas no longer sang their song. The tiny paddy frogs too had disappeared. Those trees that could had dropped their leaves, leaving bare wooden skeletons.

My thoughts were turning to winter. As I sat on my balcony one Saturday morning, supping on a can of hot coffee, I gazed longingly at the selection of rounded mountains that sat in the distance. Soon the first snows would come.

I spent that morning wandering the town's hushed, temple-dotted streets. The last of the dragonflies lay at the side of the road, dying. Grounded by dropping temperatures, their transparent, veined wings were beating far too weakly to get them airborne.

Ono has been referred to as 'little Kyoto' because the stone-paved lanes and numerous temples are said to resemble that of Japan's old capital. In fact, Ono as it is known today was built by a commander named Nagachika Kanamori some 500 years ago, who did indeed model it on Kyoto. The white wooden castle that watches over the town, adds to the effect.

I walked along a quiet strip, peering into dark little *sake* shops, which offered their brew in giant brown bottles. Ono's famously pure water means that it has a proud history of *sake* making. It is also one of the last strongholds of the *Itoyo* – a three-spined stickleback. Now a rarity in Japan, this tiny fish can only survive in the purest of water, and this is a great source of pride for the people of Ono. In fact, Ono folk love their water so much, they sometimes take bottles of it with them if they have to leave. It is, after all, Japan's third purest, as I was frequently reminded.

I stepped into a small bookshop. It was empty of people aside from the rotund lady at the till who failed to disguise her startled reaction upon seeing me enter.

I began browsing. Much of the store was devoted to *manga*, the comic book format that is as popular with *salarymen* and housewives, as it is with high school students. Rows and rows of the small paperbacks covering every genre lined the shelves. From romantic soap opera to cyborg-sci-fi, there are few topics that haven't been *manga*-ised.

Moving into the reference section I spied an intriguing book named *Herbs for Pets*. It had a photo of a Labrador eating a house plant on the front. Then I locked onto a publication that caused me even greater excitement. Entitled *Snow Mountain Fukui* the cover shot depicted one of Fukui's many peaks, snow covered and framed by a blue sky. The fact that it was entirely in Japanese did not dissuade me from handing over my yen to the lady at the till, who now seemed to have recovered from the shock of seeing a foreigner in her shop.

I headed home, clutching my new found treasure; it was to play a vital part in my Ono adventures.

***

By now, I had met all the other foreigners in the area: Americans, Canadians and one New Zealander; there were a grand total of ten. I had discovered that Brandon, a highly enthusiastic American, shared my love for snow, so I had immediately called to tell him about the book. We agreed to meet later that evening in a tiny restaurant in Katsuyama, Ono's sister town, and Brandon's adopted home.

'Seriously dude, this book is freaking awesome!' he said, as we munched on 'sauce *katsudon*', a breaded, fried pork cutlet, drenched in a barbecue-Worcestershire sauce blend.

'I can't wait for winter, man. It's gonna be sweet! I mean, all these mountains dude! And all that snow! Seriously!'

Brandon and I both agreed that we had to make use of this mountainous terrain that ringed us. We also agreed that we couldn't do it on our own. We needed a guide; someone who knew the land and could lead us safely into (and out of) Fukui's forested, bear-ridden backcountry. But we were lucky; we had received a tip-off about such a man. A man who knew the mountains of Fukui as if they were his own children. His name was Yasu. And Yasu was not only a mountaineering expert but, conveniently, also the owner of what I came to discover was the best bar in Ono (and quite possibly all of Japan).

***

Some days later, armed with the *Snow Mountain Fukui* book, Brandon and I set out to find our man of the mountains. We had been given directions and finally managed to track down his bar. Named *Yumeya*, meaning 'Dream Shop', it sat on a narrow side street at the opposite end of town to where I lived. A red awning marked its presence.

We opened the wooden door, involuntarily triggering a set of wind chimes, which announced our arrival. Heads turned, looked, then turned back again. I glanced around. On the walls hung an ice pick, a pair of snowshoes and pictures of sabre-toothed mountains. Scattered on the tables were copies of '*Hakujin* – the magazine for mountain lovers'. I nodded at Brandon; we had come to the right place.

We took a seat at the broad bar. Behind it, bottles of Japanese whisky and *shochu* were labelled with the names of regulars, handwritten in marker-pen *kanji*. A bald, bearded, smiley man appeared through a backroom door carrying a small gas burner and a plate of squid strips. He placed them in front of the two workmen sat next to us, still dressed in boots and green overalls.

'Good evening,' he said.

'Good evening,' we replied in unison.

'What can I get you?' he asked.

The bald, bearded, smiley man was Yasu, the man we had come to meet.

We each ordered a glass of Yebisu beer and sat back to admire our surroundings. An antique jukebox sat in the corner, a small TV above the bar. Tie-dyed drapes hung from the ceiling; backgammon, chess and Go were stashed on a shelf.

The workmen fired up the gas burner and the squid strips started to sizzle, producing a pungent, fishy whiff. It wasn't long before their curiosity overshadowed their shyness and they turned to ask:

'Where are you from? America?'

Without exception, white foreigners in Japan are always assumed to be American. Brandon confirmed that he was; I offered that I was from England.

'Ohhh England! David Beckham!'

I confirmed that David Beckham was also of English nationality.

'What is your job?'

We informed them of our teaching roles.

'Ohhh – teachers! Thank you,' they said with a slight bow.

They were gasmen and had spent the day digging up roads and laying new pipes. Brandon, ever eager to add to his collection of *kanji*, asked if they could jot down a few new words that had come up in our conversation. The workmen happily obliged, delighted to be teaching the teachers something.

The jingle of the wind chimes announced a new arrival. A short, skinny, forty-something man with circular 'John Lennon style' glasses entered. He plonked himself down at the bar, ordering a large Kirin beer. Seeing that we had already been engaged in conversation and were therefore safe to approach, he drew nearer. And seeing that there was a *kanji* class already in progress, decided he could also show us a thing or two about Japanese, requesting the teaching implements himself.

The workmen slid over the pen and paper. With perfect precision the new arrival carefully drew the *kanji* that made up his name, using his rudimentary English to explain that the first character meant 'Long', the second 'Peace'. Unfortunately for Long Peace, this little lesson backfired.

With the beer already taking effect, we could not pass up the immature, though comical possibilities of this name, joking that perhaps the real meaning was 'Long Piece' as in 'Large Willy', rather than 'an extended period without warfare'.

'No No No!' he protested, as we gestured crudely, leaving no room for doubt over our interpretation.

'Not long. Not long!'

On discovering I was English, he asked if I was from London.

'I was born there, but I grew up in the countryside,' I explained.

'London is very foggy,' Long Piece replied.

'Well, not really no.'

'Yes Sam *san*. My friend go to London, he say very foggy.'

'Sometimes there is some fog, but it's not normally foggy at all.'

'Yes, very foggy Sam *san*. London is very foggy,' he said, nodding solemnly.

The notion that London is permanently blanketed in fog seems to be a commonly-held belief by the Japanese and must cause great disappointment when they actually go there.

Long Piece seemed a happy man, despite his strenuous job.

'I break rocks. I take big rocks and break them into small rocks. All day breaking rocks. Very tired.'

But it emerged that he hadn't always been a rock breaker.

'Ten years before, I had design company. But then Japan's economy go down. I lost everything.'

I was later to visit his office, now an overgrown portacabin in a lay-by, and saw some of his work. He was obviously a great designer and it was sad to see his artistic talents had become redundant, now replaced by hard manual labour.

The chimes rang again. Gennai – a man who we were to discover was the bar clown – entered. The thirty-something son of a *sake* shop owner, he too joined the mêlée. Tall, shaven-headed and stubbled, he was the joker of the pack and took great amusement in our interpretation and explanation of Long Piece's name. Gennai was a real boozer; his whole life revolved around alcohol. If he wasn't selling it, he was drinking it. If he wasn't drinking it, he was recovering from drinking it. This may have explained why he was still single.

'Can you introduce me to foreign girls?' Gennai wondered hopefully.

'American or English both OK,' he confirmed.

The appearance of a man with grey, centre-parted curtains and an air of self-importance caused our companions to quieten. He was obviously a man of some status. Which was probably why he seemed disappointed that Brandon and I didn't offer a more awed reaction to his business card. Even after he pointed out his job title and tapped it with his finger for emphasis. He bought us a beer each anyway before settling his bill and striding out of the bar, submissively followed by two office ladies. Gennai informed us that the man was a high-ranking member of the local government, and that he wasn't shy in reminding people of the fact.

We worked our way through numerous brands of beer and various fishy snacks, which our newly found friends insisted on buying us. A refrigerator stood on the customer side of the bar and patrons were invited to help themselves. Bills would be settled later. Yasu stocked an impressive range of foreign beers, which made a change to Asahi, Kirin and Sapporo, the three most common in Japan. Long Piece insisted Yasu also serve us his signature dish; a most un-Japanese platter of smoked cheese. It was delicious though, even more so because Yasu smoked the cheese himself.

A reasonable level of inebriation had now been achieved all round, so Brandon and I felt the time was right to reveal the true nature of our mission. I produced my copy of the snow book and called over to Yasu. His eyes widened instantly and a smile appeared. He, of course, already owned a copy, but evidently approved of anyone else who owned it too. This was a good sign; doing our homework had paid off.

The timing was right for the next part of the plan; hoping to build our mountaineering credibility, we proudly announced that we had recently climbed Fuji. Yes, that's right, we had climbed Japan's highest mountain. What did he think of them apples? Well, not much actually. Although Gennai and Long Piece let out an exaggerated 'Ohhhh Fuji – very nice!' (the polite reaction to such a feat), Yasu wasn't so easily wowed. He had climbed it too of course, but didn't consider Japan's highest mountain to be one of its best.

'Too many people, too easy and too overrated,' he explained.

Had we blown our chance of getting a guide by revealing we were only amateur mountain appreciators? Not yet it seemed. He picked up the book and began flicking through the crisp pages, pointing out the most picturesque peaks and the best mountains for backcountry skiing. Then he disappeared into the back room, returning with a map, which he spread out over the bar. His finger enthusiastically traced the printed contours, skirting along valleys, highlighting passes and paths of Fukui's mountain ranges.

It emerged that Yasu had some pretty serious climbing experience under his belt. In his late twenties and early thirties he had climbed several Himalayan peaks in Nepal and Pakistan. We discovered he had been a local celebrity, his expeditions attracting the attention of the media. Not that he admitted this himself, but Long Piece and Gennai dismissed all his attempts at modesty, demanding he produce his scrapbook of newspaper clippings and photos.

Everything was going in the right direction. Brandon and I decided it was time to move in for the kill. Did he still climb mountains? We asked. Yes he did, although he hadn't returned to the Himalaya, and doubted he ever would. But he did still climb Japanese mountains for pleasure and occasionally for payment. Telecom companies would sometimes call upon his mountaineering expertise, employing him to lug up parts of radio antennae and satellite equipment to the summits.

But though he loved climbing mountains all year round, winter was his favourite time to climb. This was exactly the man we wanted to know.

Brandon and I volunteered that we would love to explore the mountains, if only we knew where to go. Our unsubtle hint hit its mark and finally the invite arrived. Would we like to climb with him when the snows came, he asked. Yes we would! In the meantime he would recommend some good mountains for autumn climbs – some warm ups. And would we return to his bar, he wondered? Of course, we promised. We toasted to Yasu, to the mountains and to our new friends.

We had drunk late into the night and it was time to retire. We had successfully completed our mission, securing not only the most highly qualified mountain guide in Fukui, but also one of the most useful resources a foreigner could wish for in a foreign land: a bar owner. We said our drunken goodbyes and stumbled out into the Ono dark, triggering the chimes for the final time that evening.

I kept my promise. Yasu, Long Piece, Gennai and various others from Yumeya's colourful cast were to become regular fixtures in my life. It was a place to drink and be merry with the everyday townsfolk of Ono, from monks to musicians. A place I would happily go on my own of an evening to sit, chat, practise my Japanese and eat smoked cheese.

I knew I would never be a true local in Japan, but Yumeya would become the one place that I managed to feel like one. And with Yasu to lead us, the adventures into Fukui's deserted mountains would soon begin.

Chapter 8
Green Tea and Cake with Keiko

The rain was falling softly as I drove to work. Hiding behind dense mist, the mountains were nowhere to be seen. I passed a high school girl piloting her bike with one hand whilst holding an umbrella with the other. Her skirt rode high, revealing what must have been cold legs.

Zooming up to the traffic lights, I had to brake sharply as they turned red. I had developed a hatred for Ono's road signals. Those responsible for the town's highways and byways had managed to install a set of lights at almost every single junction, even those whose peak rush-hour traffic consisted of a tractor and two bikes. Thus, I was normally left drumming my wheel impatiently, waiting for non-existent vehicles to pass.

I arrived at school, stepped into the foyer and swapped my outdoor shoes for my indoor pair. As I walked towards the staff room, the smell of a petrol station hit me and I saw a row of plastic paraffin cans, neatly aligned in the corridor.

'This time the kids have gone too far,' I thought.

I knew there were some troublemakers about, but surely dousing the place in paraffin and burning it down was beyond even class 2-1. But arson was not on the agenda. The cans contained fuel for the school's antiquated heaters; indeed, paraffin is the scent of winter in Japan. Looking like Daleks from Doctor Who, one stood in the corner of each classroom. Belching out a few calories of smelly warmth, they toasted those sat close, whilst students at the back of the class received little benefit. However, the biggest surprise was that it was the students who were tasked with keeping them topped up with fuel. The fact that thirteen-year-olds were trusted with highly flammable liquids struck me as a strong sign of faith but was typical of the responsibility that is placed on Japanese children from a young age.

The rain drummed down all day. Despite the wet weather, I still went walking with Shiro, my canine friend. She didn't seem to mind the wet and neither did I. Armed with my brolly and wellies, we tramped off over the muddy baseball pitch and past the rusting railway carriage that served as the school shed.

Under the now-skeletal cherry trees we went and onto the quiet road. Gone were the pea-coloured paddies; the land had taken on a dull, drab palette, now muddy and bare. I relished the smell of the rain-dampened landscape and I breathed deep, delighting in the earthy, grassy scent. Except for the hiss of rain, the land was silent, lending a quiet calm to the day.

Preparations for winter had already begun. Corrugated sheets of plastic and metal were lent up against the houses; snow shields to deflect the soon-to-come whiteness and keep a life line from front door to road, open. But what really intrigued me were the trees.

If Britain is a nation of dog lovers, Japan is a nation of tree lovers. Almost every shrub, bush and hedge that I passed had been strung up, boarded over or secured with intricate webbing to protect boughs and branches from the damaging weight of the impending snow. From little bonsai to large pines that had great bamboo wigwams built to protect them, none was left to fend alone. It was a practice I thought a little unnecessary but then the locals were very fond of their trees. They spent so much time preening, pruning and grooming them, that perhaps the bond between man and tree is greater in Japan than anywhere else in the world.

I embarked on my normal circuit, which took me through the paddies and under a large blue road sign, left to Ono City, right to Hokyoji Temple. I took a right. The rain murmured as it splashed down in the muddy fields. I passed a small graveyard, its polished granite stones shining in the wet. They were deeply cut with *kanji* of the dead; fresh flowers lay at their base. I stopped at the lone vending machine that sat outside a small workshop and bought a *genki* drink.

Shiro stopped straining on her lead and looked up at me, her ears pricked and head cocked to one side, as if to say:

'Go on, give me some! Please!'

'No Shiro! *Genki* drinks are not for dogs,' I told her.

Indeed, the hefty shot of caffeine gave my bowels a nudge and within five minutes of swallowing the fluorescent liquid, I felt a rapid movement inside. Pulling a 180 with the hound, I made a hurried return to the school.

Japan is famous for its toilets. Everyone has heard about their futuristic toilet technology with computerised control panels that operate nozzles, play music, have heated (or even air conditioned) seats, shoot water into all sorts of places and even blow dry your parts. But what many might not realise is that such 'Super Toilets' are not yet the norm. They tend only to be found in hotels or private homes. Certainly, neither my apartment, nor either of my schools had any such luxury, so it was the more standard squatter toilet over which I now crouched.

Back in the UK, it is fair to say that a trip to the loo is, by and large, a pleasant experience. Sitting on the porcelain throne for a while could only be described as a relaxing way to spend some time. A chance to catch up on some reading perhaps, something that might even be looked forward to. This is not so with the Japanese squatter. There is no comfy seat, no relaxing whilst you make your deposit. Instead, you spend a precarious period hunched over a hole, wearing ill-fitting toilet slippers, trying to maintain perfect balance. It's a real test of thigh muscle and far from relaxing. There's no sitting around reading; you get in and out as fast as possible. Overall, it was an experience that I'd rather not have to repeat. Unfortunately, I had to. Every day.

There was also the matter of smell. I had noticed a slight change in the fragrance of my deposits since I arrived in Japan. Whilst I don't claim they have ever smelled of roses, I am fairly sure the aroma had taken a turn for the worst. Diet may have been one cause, but the fact that there is no water in the bowl to envelop and contain the consignment is probably the primary reason. After dropping the kids off, I would look down and think: 'I just don't know you anymore'.

I returned to the staff room to find I had walked right into the middle of some severe disciplinary action. In Japan, unlike Britain, discipline is seen more to be the responsibility of the school than the parents. Some school rules apply to students even outside of school hours. Though corporal punishment is no longer permitted, light physical punishment seemed to be acceptable; teachers often used a book to tap the head of a student who wasn't paying attention, a practice that would probably elicit a law suit in Britain or America these days.

Normally, Japanese schools have one or two teachers who take on the role of official disciplinarians. In my school, it was the PE teacher, whom the kids had learned to fear. Atypically large and muscular for a Japanese person, he towered over the students and was the tallest member of staff. Here, he was now in disciplinarian mode, and it was a fearsome experience that made me feel surprisingly uneasy, so it must have been particularly unpleasant for the lad on the receiving end.

The student was made to sit on the floor in *seiza*, a kneeling position used during certain rituals and martial arts, which becomes quite uncomfortable after a while. The teacher then stood over him and proceeded to bellow. His tone undulated from a high note to a low growl. It projected an aggressive, threatening and unnerving quality, like an engine being slowly and menacingly revved up and down.

I couldn't understand much of what was being said, but like a dog gets the gist by the tone of voice without comprehending the actual words, I knew this student was in for a rough time. After five minutes, I was relieved to be able to leave the room – I had a class to teach – but when I returned fifty minutes later, the student was still sitting in *seiza*, tears rolling down his cheeks. He was a particularly troublesome boy who frequently misbehaved in my classes but on this occasion, I couldn't help feeling sorry for him.

However, my pity didn't last for long. It was 4:30 and my working day was almost done. And tonight, I had an important date with my new found Japanese family. After several months of orphanage, I had finally been adopted.

***

Following my wisdom tooth troubles some weeks ago, the kindly Tomiko who had assisted me had managed to convince her sister in law – Keiko – that being a friend to a foreigner was not that bad after all. I had been keen to find someone to help me learn more Japanese, and Keiko had loosely agreed to teach me.

It was 6:30pm on the dot when I arrived at Keiko's house. I had made special attention to my timeliness of late, especially when it was a case of first impressions. The house was beautiful; a traditional building with wooden walls and charcoal-grey tiles on a roof that curled at the ends. I pressed the door bell, setting off a musical chime.

'*Irashaimaseee*! (Welcome!)' emanated from inside.

I stood outside waiting.

'*Irashaimaseee! Dozo, dozo!* (Welcome, come in, come in!)' I heard again.

I remained outside not wanting to let myself in in case it appeared rude. Then the door slid open and Keiko's kindly face greeted me. I slipped off my shoes and placed them neatly together, facing the door. No one ever leaves their shoes untidily in Japan, apart from foreigners. When I had done so in the past, by the time I came to put them on again, someone would have rearranged them neatly together. There was some zen wisdom that I later saw in Fukui's Eiheiji temple that helps explain the reasons for such shoe etiquette:

Illumination from Our Feet
Arranging our shoes neatly,
We bring harmony to our minds

When our minds are harmonious,
We arrange our shoes neatly
If we arrange shoes neatly when we take them off
Our minds won't be disturbed when we put them on
If someone leaves shoes in disarray
Let us silently put them to order
Such an act will surely bring harmony
To the minds of people around the world

I stepped up onto the shiny, wooden floor and presented Keiko with my *omiyage* – (my gift) – a box of English fudge. Gift-giving is especially important in Japan, and small edible treats from one's home country or region are not just appreciated, but expected. Keiko took the box, thanked me, and ushered me into her lounge, a medium-sized room with a raised platform at one side, which housed black and white family photographs. Inside a cupboard was the magnificent family shrine.

'*Dozo* Sam *san*,' said Keiko, beckoning me to sit down on a cushion.

'*Arigatou*,' I thanked, lowering myself to the *tatami* floor.

Keiko then slipped through the door and returned with the rest of the family. One by one, we went through the introductions, which involved bowing, a 'pleased to meet you' and, in the interest of cultural exchange, a handshake.

The Tanakas were a typical middle-class Japanese family unit. Keiko was the professional house wife who counted cook, cleaner and Chief Financial Officer of the household amongst her duties. She was also responsible for the care of her mother-in-law, a frail elderly lady, who said very little, but still had a smile for me. She sat on a special chair rather than the floor.

Mr Tanaka was tallish with glasses, swept-back hair and was an archetypal *salaryman*. He worked for a car corporation in a city more than an hour away and hence had to leave early each morning and rarely returned before nine or ten at night.

The Tanakas had two children. A son who lived and worked in Nagoya and didn't say much apart from the pleasantries, and Yuko, their confident and pretty twenty-two-year-old daughter, with long hair as black and shiny as obsidian.

As soon as everyone was seated on the thin cushions at the low table, the meal commenced. Keiko had laid on a real feast; it began with plates of pickled, sliced vegetables and sweet potatoes, then came *sashimi*, little bowls of soy and *wasabi*, grated radish, a pot of bubbling stew in the centre of the table and numerous items that I couldn't identify but ate anyway.

Beer, wine and *sake* flowed freely. Keiko and Mr Tanaka both spoke some English and I had by now acquired enough Japanese to enable rudimentary conversation, so we spoke in a mixture of languages. Where we stumbled, Keiko's electronic dictionary, and Yuko, who was a trainee English teacher, helped bridge the gaps. Soon we were all laughing and joking (apart from the son who stayed rather subdued) as we dug into each other's life stories.

Mr Tanaka was a fan of Scotch whisky and dreamed of going to Scotland one day. Keiko played ping-pong once a week and liked to sketch. Yuko had a collection of 'Hello Kitty' mobile phone trinkets, which she had amassed since she was a teenager; she hoped to eventually complete the collection by acquiring each of the forty-seven different Kittys that had been created for Japan's forty-seven prefectures. And the son, well, the son didn't say much. He ate and drank, but remained silent for the entire evening.

Just when I thought the meal was over, Keiko would disappear and return with a new set of dishes. By the end, we each must have eaten from fifteen different pieces of crockery and glassware; I was glad I wasn't doing the washing up. To round off the evening, Keiko poured green tea and we all sat back in a happy stupor. It was getting late, and it was a school night; Mr Tanaka had a frightfully early start and Yuko had to study for an exam. I thanked them sincerely for the lovely evening, bowed and wished them good night. They watched me climb into the taxi, Mr Tanaka sternly ensuring that the driver knew exactly where he was to take me before letting us depart.

I would spend almost every Wednesday for the next two years with Keiko, adding Japanese phrases to my collection, deciphering *kanji* and drinking green tea. The following summer I would embark on adventures in Fukui backwaters with Yuko, and Mr Tanaka and I were to sip whisky together on several occasions. Yes, the Tanaka family was to become a vital part of my life in Japan, taking their 'foreign son' dutifully into their lives to share their language, culture and customs.

As I sat in the car in a satisfied *sake* haze, I noted the cloud had cleared from the mountain tops. A dusting of snow on the highest peaks was just visible in the starlight; winter was on its way.

Chapter 9
Encapsulated

Before I knew it, the Christmas holidays arrived. I decided to spend New Year in Hong Kong, visiting a friend who had ditched his native Scotland for this tiny Asian territory. And who could blame him? Scotland may have its bonny lassies and lots of lochs but as my friend explained, Hong Kong was much more suitable for someone with a strong affinity for Asian ladies.

I sat down in the reception of the apartment block I had booked for us and surveyed the paraphernalia surrounding me; large glass jars full of dried plants, dried mushrooms and dried seahorses sat on the shelves. It transpired that the manager was also a doctor practicing Chinese medicine and was busy performing acupuncture on the middle-aged man in the corner of the room. Perhaps worried that we might take our business elsewhere if he didn't hurry, he appeared from behind the curtain, revealing his pin-cushioned patient, and took to the more pressing task at hand: lightening our wallets.

After this had been achieved and we had surrendered our passports, we were led to our room. We traipsed along a long corridor of grotty-looking flats that resembled prison cells on account of the metal grilles that covered their doors. A slightly uneasy feeling rose in our stomachs. Why would you need metal bars over your front door? I suddenly recalled something I had read in the *Rough Guide* about a dodgy block of apartments in this area, which was full of junkies and was regularly raided by the police. I was now wondering if I had booked us in for a one-week stay at Hotel Heroin. Come to think of it, the room had been pretty good value.

'It looked OK on the website...' I tried to assure my girlfriend as we walked deeper into the tower block building. She had gone very quiet, an almost unheard of occurrence.

We finally reached our very own cell, unlocked the grille and then the actual door too. A pair of single beds sat below a little window and in the corner was the tiniest toilet/basin/shower room I had ever seen, which is saying something when you live in Japan. It was so small that I later had a shower whilst sitting on the toilet.

We dumped our bags on the floor and collapsed onto the thin mattresses in silence. My girlfriend burst into tears.

'It's horrible!' she sobbed.

I had to admit, it had looked better on the website. Still, it was clean, cheap and central, and her tears soon dried up when she realised our close proximity to several high-class shoe shops.

***

Aside from our jail cell accommodation, I loved Hong Kong with its splice of exotic East yet familiar West. Antique, double-decker trams, tall and narrow, whizzed through streets overshadowed by high-rise malls selling designer labels from the world's top fashion houses. But just a couple of blocks behind, tanks of fish, bowls of crabs, buckets of clams, cages of huge frogs and boxes of tortoises were on sale in the street markets.

I watched with grim fascination a live turtle having its shell hacked off with a machete; a large eel being cut in half and put on display still writhing violently. Fish plucked from their tank, chopped into thirds and sold still quivering. Some people weren't even bothering to have their supper killed. They simply selected a fish and took it home live in a plastic bag. Several large fish had managed to leap from their tanks only to find themselves flapping in the gutter, while people passed by unperturbed. Chickens' feet, a Chinese favourite, sat on trays; goats' and pigs' heads hung from meat hooks.

Everything was either live, or very recently deceased. It was somewhat barbaric to watch but this is because in the West all this slaughtering goes on behind closed doors, thus removing us from the killing and falsely sanitising the meat and fish we eat.

Aside from this market, which was most certainly not suitable for vegetarians, the most memorable part of my stay was New Year's Day. The weather had been unusually cold; so cold that a ground frost had formed in some parts of the territory, which had caused great excitement for the city's residents. All the TV channels were covering the 'Frost Phenomenon'. It made me chuckle to see reporters interviewing people who had risen early, especially to witness this rare occurrence. They enthusiastically recounted the scene, with the joy of a child who has just discovered snow.

***

After an excellent week, it was time to return to Japan. As I sat in Hong Kong airport lounge, I found myself looking forward to going 'home'. I had been in Japan for only six months but already it was really beginning to feel very homely. Once on board the plane it was bizarrely comforting to be back in the bubble; back to hearing only rapid-fire Japanese again and not understanding most of what was being said. I found myself at ease being the only foreigner on the plane; it felt normal.

Yes, I was definitely looking forward to being back in Japan. Looking forward to being back in Japan, that was, until we landed in Japan, and I went through Nagoya customs. As I approached the final barrier between me and my temporary homeland, an eager officer who had previously been in some form of stasis, spied me and sparked into life. He stood tall, chest puffed out, and beckoned me to walk through his aisle.

How nice to be back in a country where the people are so friendly, I thought, as I shuffled along with my fellow Japanese passengers. But I was soon to be harshly reminded that I was still just a lone white buoy in a sea of sushi. What I thought was a welcoming smile, was in fact a

'I've caught myself a *gaijin*!' smirk. I handed him my passport. He eyeballed my visa. Then the questioning commenced.

'Where have you been?'

'Hong Kong,' I told him politely, knowing full well that he knew full well that everyone in the queue had come from Hong Kong.

'Where are you from?'

'Britain.' As was clearly stated in my passport he held in his hand.

'What you do in Japan?'

'I'm an English teacher.' As noted on my visa which he was staring at.

'What's in your bag?'

'Clothes,' I said, hoping this was all just some routine role play, some security show for the benefit of the post-9/11 administration, and that he would then let me pass. But he didn't let me pass; he wasn't finished with me yet. He ducked under his desk and resurfaced with a laminated A4 sheet.

'Do you have these in your bag?' he asked, handing the sheet to me.

I looked at it carefully. Depicted in full colour were photographs of marijuana, ecstasy tablets, cocaine, a gun and some bullets.

'No. No I don't. Absolutely not.' I assured him seriously, shaking my head rapidly from side to side in a bid to convince him that I wasn't a drugs or weapons smuggler.

But it wasn't enough. As every other Japanese passenger on that plane strode through security without even eliciting a single question from the officers, I was led to a door signed 'Special Investigation' to be investigated, specially.

In the small, brightly lit room, an older, more senior-looking officer was waiting. When I saw a torch, I began to worry how special the investigation was going to be. The junior officer then produced again the laminated sheet with the pictures of marijuana, ecstasy tablets, cocaine, a gun and some bullets, and asked again if I had any of them in my bag, on the off chance that I had managed to buy some on the way from the security desk.

For the second time I affirmed that I did not possess any of the said items. He told me to sit down; I did. Then, under the glare of Senior, Junior opened my bag and began to pull out its insides, eagerly disgorging its contents onto the table. Out came my crumpled t-shirts, tops and trousers. My socks, shorts and shoes. Every pocket of every garment was investigated and Junior seemed to be enjoying himself. He was definitely taking pleasure in rifling through my belongings, occasionally confirming the identity of items for which he knew the English. He was desperate to uncover some marijuana, some ecstasy tablets, some cocaine, a gun or, at the very least, a few bullets.

'DVD?'
'Yes DVD.'
'CD?'
'Yes CD.'
'Book?'
'No, it's a surface to air missile that runs on a cocktail of marijuana, ecstasy tablets and cocaine – of course it's a bloody book!' I thought, irked at his pointless questions, which were obviously designed to show off his rudimentary English skills in front of Senior.

Sadly for Junior, he didn't find any of the items on his wish list. But he did find something that gave him great pleasure in examining and caused me some embarrassment.

I had spied something in a Chinese medicine shop in down town Hong Kong that I just couldn't resist buying. A small box containing a slim, silver canister of a potion called 'Pink Point Sexual Oil'. Apparently a 'Royal Prescription for Chinese Emperors of Successive Dynasties', it contained '10% Gecko' and '7% Dear Penis' amongst other ingredients. Understand that I bought it for the sole reason that its label amused me and it would make a great souvenir. Junior however saw fit to closely scrutinise the *Karma Sutra*-style illustration and even Senior felt it was a matter that warranted his more experienced eye.

Junior looked up at me with a grin and asked:

'Sexual play oil?'

'Erm . . . something like that,' I said, embarrassed and now quite peeved at the invasion of my privacy.

Ironically, when it came to the only thing in my bag that might have landed me in trouble, Junior didn't even give it a second look. Many medical drugs that are legal in other countries are banned in Japan; I had some hay fever tablets that I suspected contained an illegal substance but he paid no attention at all to my small collection of medicines.

I admit the whole episode annoyed me. It had been a long day, weariness was kicking in and I just wanted to sleep. I had been singled out for this special treatment, purely because I was not Japanese and I was also worried that I would miss the last bus into town. My flight had already arrived late, and this further hold-up could end up costing me an expensive taxi trip. But I was to have the last laugh. After Junior was finally (dis)satisfied that I had no marijuana, ecstasy tablets, cocaine, guns or bullets, he then had the task of folding all my clothes away neatly and repacking.

As this was the first time I had ever been searched at an airport, I was unfamiliar with the protocol that a suspected drug and weapons trafficker is supposed to perform. Do you assist in the repacking of your belongings? I wasn't sure, so I just sat there quietly watching him folding my garments, including my dirty underwear, which he halved and quartered expertly. Even Senior pitched in. At this point I asked politely if I might take a photo of the two officers, boxer shorts in hand; alas, permission was denied. But at least the latex gloves had never materialised.

After half an hour I was released without charge and with a mad dash, managed to catch the last bus into the city. It deposited me on to the cold streets of Nagoya where I set out in search of one of the most Japanese of all creations, the capsule hotel.

***

With the help of the white-gloved taxi driver, I eventually located the multi-storey building that housed the hotel. My first error was to stride straight up to the reception desk. I was immediately asked to return to the foyer and remove my shoes. I meekly obeyed, returning to the desk with my shoes in hand, which he exchanged for a pair of slippers. I then asked for a bed again, but was pointed in the direction of a vending machine. Tired and confused, I slunk over to it, and piecing together the Japanese, realised I had to pay at the machine. I fed some yen into its mouth; it spat out at little white ticket. I took this over to the man on reception who then, finally, exchanged it for a key; a key to what I hoped would be a good night's slumber.

I stepped out of the lift on to the 7th floor and followed the signs for the bedroom. I was confronted by a scene that could have been straight out of an intergalactic sci-fi film. Two rows of double-decker, cream-coloured, plastic-moulded pods disappeared into the distance. I was on a battle star-ship set for hyperspace. I would crawl into my stasis unit to be transported to a galaxy, far, far away. This is the coolest thing I have ever seen, I thought.

I stashed my luggage in the locker matching my key and walked down the long corridor, finally locating my allotted pod; it was on the upper 'floor'. I climbed the three stainless steel steps and crawled in. A television, radio, alarm clock and reading light were all built in to the pre-fabricated cubicle. A shallow ledge acted as a shelf; scars of caramelised plastic revealed where lit cigarettes had been rested too long.

I jumped down, going in search of the bathroom. It was fitted out in aging eighties decor, but clean and tidy. I nodded to the man who was shaving over a sink and helped myself to a free disposable toothbrush. After searching all the other shelves and cupboards, I could find no toothpaste. I resigned myself to the fact I would have to do without, cursing the Japanese for their lack of dental hygiene. Seconds later, I was praising the Japanese for their ingenuity; the brush came pre-impregnated with the optimum dose of minty-cool paste.

Back in the pod, I pulled down the woven rattan screen. There were no doors; the blind would be the only barrier between me and all the other pod-dwellers, and as I was to learn, one-millimetre thick rattan isn't a renowned sound barrier. Although it was past midnight and I was completely shattered, I flicked on the TV. There was only one channel. It was showing Japanese porn, which I found blurs out any offending parts, so all you can see are two naked people (sometimes more), whose genitalia don't wish to be identified. This failed to turn on my already frazzled brain, so I turned off and laid my head on the pillow. It was small, uncomfortable and seemed to be filled with hard, dried beans.

I tried to fall asleep but despite my fatigue, sleep would not come. The pod was hot and stuffy and the air conditioning, which spewed from an aeroplane-style nozzle, came on only sporadically. Then I became aware of my roommates. Grunts, snores, coughs and the muffled sound of blurred porn echoed around the room. I was in for a long night.

Eventually, I did manage to drop off. Unfortunately, I only discovered that this must have happened when I was awoken by a bunch of noisy drunks, who came in talking and laughing loudly. I then spent the rest of the night clock-watching, urging the morning to come. As soon as 6am arrived I exited my sweaty pod, to find that almost all of my fellow pod-dwellers had already done so, and jumped in the lift.

I exchanged my key for my shoes at the front desk and joined the rush hour throng headed for Nagoya station. I was glad to be out and just a few hours from my very own *futon*.

***

A night in a capsule hotel is certainly a unique and almost iconic Japanese experience. But it wasn't one that I would be rushing to repeat (though I was to stay in several more before I left Japan). Being in your own pod tricks you into thinking you have your own zone, but you are still sharing a room with fifty other men. Nevertheless, they are an ingenious use of space, a symbol of Japan's love for miniaturisation, and the cheapest bed you'll find in a Japanese city.

Chapter 10
Adventures in Snow

Few outside of the snow sports fraternity realise that Japan is a Mecca for skiing. Indeed, there seems to be a misconception amongst the West that Japan is a year-round hot, tropical country, rather than one that has over 500 ski resorts and receives some of the heaviest snowfalls in the world.

Though it was not my only reason for wanting to visit the land of sumo and sushi, the tales of incredible snowfalls certainly played their part in my decision to venture to Japan. In fact, when it came to selecting somewhere in Japan to spend the next two years of my life, snow was the only thing I had on my mind.

My research had consisted of calculating which prefectures had the most ski resorts and the highest snowfalls. It was armed with this information that I had applied to live and work on the northern island of Hokkaido (first choice) and Nagano prefecture (second choice), both of which boasted Winter Olympic fame and were renowned as the best that Japan had to offer when it came to snow.

However, destiny had other plans. I had been posted to Fukui, a place not known for its snow sports excellence, in fact, a place seemingly not known for much at all, apart from accidents at one of its fifteen nuclear power stations. But little did I know that the Japanese snow gods had big plans for me. After worrying about missing out on Japan's renowned powder, I would experience a winter with snowfalls so heavy that trains would be derailed, houses would be crushed and over 100 people would perish in its icy grip.

***

Before even drawing back the curtains, I could tell it had come. The glow that spilled from the window betrayed its presence; the snow had arrived. A joyous euphoria welled up inside. I eased on my slippers and stepped on to the balcony. Yesterday, the land had been dull and dark. Now the rice paddies and mountains glittered with a gilt of white gold. Despite being a grown man with twenty-five years under my belt, snow still fills me with the breathless excitement of a child. Even the most uninspiring landscapes are transformed to scenes of sheer splendour by applying a glaze of snow. Nature's foundation, snow covers all acne and scars, creating the perfect complexion.

I decided to skip breakfast. I was too excited to eat and it would take me extra time to uncover my car and escape from the car park anyway. I grabbed the brand new aluminium shovel that had been waiting patiently for this day, stepped into my wellington boots, and out into the snow. It was already shin deep and squeaked satisfyingly as I trudged over to the vending machine to get my normal can of hot coffee.

I began to shovel. The snow was light and soft and it took me fifteen minutes to clear a path to the road. I switched my car to 4x4 mode and exited the parking lot. As I drove cautiously along the snow-covered roads, I began to regret missing breakfast, so pulled into a 'Familymart' store. The refrigerated shelves were stocked with sushi boxes and the Japanese version of a sandwich (which has been lost in translation somewhat). But I needed something hot so I headed for the counter. A stainless steel water bath sat on the counter, steaming. It looked like something I would have used back in the lab. But it didn't contain conical flasks or centrifuge tubes. It contained *oden* – a popular winter food consisting of triangles of the bland, gelatinous *konnyaku*, parcels of processed fish, and *daikon*, a vegetable that when boiled, smells and tastes like a fart.

I had already ascertained that *oden* (and in particular *oden daikon*) was my least favourite Japanese food, so I asked for a *'kare mahn'* instead – a deliciously doughy dumpling filled with curry sauce.

***

I was at my desk in the staff room when the electrical snow storm began. It was midday but the sun had vanished, leaving a darkened, moody, gunmetal grey sky. Thunder started to growl in the distance. Lightning flashed from afar. But the rumble neared as the storm enveloped us, and soon became an explosion, with cracks so loud that I would have been frightened if I wasn't so excited.

Then came the snow. So much snow. Great big, fat flakes the size of Pringles, swirling and whirling as the blizzard took hold. It continued all day. By the time I left work, it took me another fifteen minutes to clear the snow from my car. I drove back home, carefully negotiating the snowy roads. Ploughs were working hard and the sprinklers that sprayed water into the roads (a bizarre though surprisingly effective method of snow clearance) were also assisting.

I went to bed watching the flakes fall. Swarms upon swarms of white moths coming to smother the land. Their bodies dropping to the ground, layer upon layer upon layer, suffocating and smoothing over the earth.

The following morning it was still snowing heavily. Half a metre now lay on the ground. My wellington boots were no longer high enough to keep the snow out. I spent thirty minutes clearing a path from my car to the road. The tarmac had long since been covered, but at least the snow had been compacted.

All day long, the snow continued, all the while the drifts grew. The flakes were like feathers. Big, soft and coming in such numbers. Imagine an enormous pillow exploding in the sky, and all the white feathers floating to earth.

After two days of continuous snowfall, cars that had not been cleared were just bumps in the snowscape. By the fourth day of the storm, giant walls of snow had appeared on the roadsides where ploughs had carved canyons. These dwarfed the pedestrians who were now forced to walk on the road as the pavements had disappeared.

By day six, all but the most vital roads became completely impassable. The clearance teams were unable to keep up with the snowy onslaught; there was simply nowhere left to put the snow.

By day eight, the whole of Fukui had ground to a halt under the weight of the white. Neither car, train nor plane could leave the prefecture.

We were completely shut off, cocooned by the snow.

***

School had switched to the winter timetable. The whole day was set back by twenty minutes, allowing extra time to dig out cars and drive on snowy roads. Most of my colleagues constantly grumbled about the snow.

'I don't like snow Sam *san*. I must get up early to clear my car.' said the maths teacher.

'Yes, we must also clear the roofs of our houses.' added the school nurse.

Growing up with such heavy winters had left them completely loveless for snow. For them it just meant miserable cold, constant inconvenience and endless shovelling as they struggled to keep their car parks and roofs clear. But for me, with my childlike love of snow, it was a winter of dreams. I'd lived in Whistler, Canada, I'd seen the mountains of New Zealand and visited the French Alps and Andorran Pyrenees, but never, ever, had I realised that snow in such great volumes could exist. I found it hard to believe that the sky could contain so much snow, but I had no complaints; I was in white paradise.

I loved the snow so much, that I actually looked forward to coming home from work and spending two or three hours shovelling, scraping, chipping and digging away the snow to keep our car park open. Not that it made much of a dent. I would recruit my neighbours, Chris, a big, burly, bear of an American, and Luke, a tall, spectacled Welshmen, and the three of us would spend an evening toiling to clear our cars and exit route. But we would always wake up the following morning to find a fresh two feet on the ground, locking us in like a cold white prison.

After a couple of weeks, several of the residents of our apartment block gave up. Believing the fight was futile, they simply left their cars to become buried, planning to dig them out again weeks later when the weather warmed.

I however continued to dig; it was almost a matter of survival. The entrance to our apartment block was under threat from being sealed off from the outside world. Every day, upon opening my front door, I would be confronted by the ever advancing 'glacier' that would creep inwards. Only daily shovelling kept our life line open.

That night at my favourite bar – Yumeya – Yasu told me it was like a 'winter of old'. The older patrons nodded knowingly as they sipped steaming *sake* from little cups. When they were children, the snow fell so deeply that the ground floors of their houses became completely buried they told me.

The only way they could get in or out was via their balconies.

***

I was eager to explore the frozen world I was now living in and so began a mission to visit all of Fukui's ski areas after school and at weekends.

The snow was hurrying down from the night sky as I drove towards Kadohara's tiny *suki-jo* (ski area). I felt like an arctic explorer as I excitedly wove my way up the white roads, braving the storm, when few others dared leave their homes. The route was completely covered. Black tarmac had become white snowpack. My headlights couldn't penetrate far into the mass of whirling flakes but my four-wheel drive Suzuki Wagon kept me on track as I passed through the giant red gate that spanned the road above the Kuzuryu river gorge. A little further on, I drove by a huddle of homes now snuggled under a thick duvet of snow, before pulling into Kadohara ski area's empty car park.

I stepped out of my car into a deep drift. The slopes were bathed in the sodium glow of floodlights. I expected total silence, but instead, muffled Japanese pop music – J-Pop – floated over the airwaves from the ski area's PA system. Puzzled by the lack of people, I donned my gear anyway and trudged to a ramshackle hut to buy a ski ticket. I tried to ask the young lift attendant where everyone was but he just shrugged. Either my attempt at a literal translation made no sense, or he was also at a loss as to why not a single other person had ventured out to ski the exceptionally snowy conditions.

I clambered aboard the rickety two-man lift, which rumbled me to the top through ever-falling flakes. As I stepped off and sat down to strap on my board, I saw that not a single other track was present. The snow was completely untouched; the entire mountain was mine. I had never been so privileged. I set off through the deep, deep snow, greedily devouring this local delicacy. My board hissed as it glided over the surface, parting the crystals and spurting smoky waves of snow into the air as I made big, slow turns in the pillow-soft powder.

The air was so full of flakes, I couldn't help breathing snow. The pines groaned as I passed, as if to complain about the ever increasing burden they were being forced to bear. Three lifties watched from the cosy glow of their wooden huts. They loyally dashed into the storm to dust the snow from the lift seat and bow to me each time I lapped them, but they were in for a quiet shift. I was their only customer that evening.

In the world of winter sports there is a saying: 'no friends on a powder day'. Light, fluffy, powder snow is considered the premium form of all snow conditions, so the saying means that when powder snow is on offer, you don't hang around waiting for lagging friends; instead you make the most of this rare commodity. But that night at Kadohara, the phrase took on a new meaning. Here I was, with snow falling so fast and thick that my tracks were being covered almost as quickly as I could make them, yet it seemed no one else was willing to join me on that snow-stormy January night.

***

I was now living in a place that got more snow in ten days than England gets in ten years, and I wanted to make the most of it. I had discovered the existence of the school cross-country ski club back in summer, and had been eagerly anticipating the start of the winter. Now the time had come for me to add a new string to my snow bow.

At 3:30pm lessons finished and I excitedly made my way to ski club's HQ, a small, wooden shed that sat just beyond the now frozen *koi* pond. Rows of the ankle-high boots, toothpick-thin skis and long, light-weight poles lined the walls of the hut. The students seemed happy to have me join their club, but they did have a pressing concern. It was well known that all foreigners have massive, foreign-sized feet; would they be able to find ski boots big enough to accommodate mine? To their surprise, a suitable fit was found and we were soon trudging over the snow, kitted up, and en route to the school ski trails.

After a few warm-up stretches, I clipped on the skis and set off. I thought the transition from one plank to two would be easy, but it seemed that my six years of snowboarding experience counted for nothing. My first attempts at moving just saw me flailing around. I fell over repeatedly and, when I was on my feet, I resembled a newly born giraffe. This was of great amusement to the students. Most of them were already proficient cross-country skiers and shot off, gliding over the trails that had been carved out over the baseball pitch and surrounding rice paddies, now buried under almost a metre of snow.

Though my Japanese was improving all the time, it remained insufficient for me to understand the finer details of cross-country skiing technique as relayed by Takeuchi *sensei*, the club supervisor, so I had to teach myself. Over the coming weeks I picked up enough to wobble my way around the circuit and despite frequent falls, the ski club soon became the highlight of my day. I couldn't wait to clip on the skis and practise my stride. Even when it was snowing so hard that the club was cancelled, I would venture out alone anyway, goggles on, hood up, and try my hardest to improve my *kuro-kan* ability. It was a full body workout, but in a gymnasium that could never be rivalled by a sweaty room full of fancy treadmills and exercise bikes.

I spent as much time as possible on the ski circuit, practising my Japanese and my skiing, chatting and joking with the students. Admittedly, my technique never became entirely polished (by the end of the winter I was still getting lapped by thirteen-year-old girls) but I didn't care. I was content just to ski over the white paddy plateau under the eyes of the soft, wooded mountains.

***

Winter continued and the snow kept coming. Nights were cold. Despite the onslaught of freezing weather and heavy snow that would fall every year, the apparent bad design of the local buildings was an ongoing mystery to me. Although Japan is hailed as one of the most technologically advanced nations in the world, the vast majority of the buildings in Fukui, including houses and schools seemed ill-equipped to cope with the extreme climate.

My apartment had single-glazed windows that were large and draughty. My front door was made of steel, a material not known for its insulating properties. Woven straw *tatami* mats certainly look fancy, but don't keep feet warm like a plush carpet would. I had no central heating system; my only sources of warmth were my two paraffin heaters. These did belch out fumy, smelly heat, but when your internal walls are made of paper, any heat you do manage to muster doesn't hang around for long.

I imagine the conversation between two Japanese architects might go something like this:

Architect 1: 'Our country is one of harsh climatic extremes. In summer it is hot and humid, yet in winter it is sub-zero with heavy snow.'

Architect 2: 'Then how shall we design our homes to protect us from the elements and create comfortable living spaces?'

Architect 1: 'This is indeed a difficult problem but I have an idea. Let us build our homes with no insulation, no central heating, and no double glazing.'

Architect 2: 'Yes, this is surely the best way to ensure the comfort of our people.'

Due to the fumes, paraffin heaters cannot be left on all night, so sleeping was particularly chilly. I slept not just fully clothed, but with an extra hooded top on, inside a sleeping bag, under a duvet and pinned by a weighty assortment of additional blankets. I may have prevented hypothermia, but still I was cold. The thermometer that sat inside my kitchen reached a low of four degrees centigrade numerous times that winter. But I had it warm compared to others. My friend Lewis, who lived in an older and draftier home, frequently witnessed freezing point inside his abode.

Given the lack of adequate central heating systems, many people in Japan take a more local approach to keeping warm. For example, small, disposable warmers called *kairo* can be adhered to any part of the body and provide a few hours of warmth. In Japanese households and some traditional restaurants, a heated table called a *kotatsu* is a favourite weapon of warmth and those who have a Western-style toilet may also have the pleasure of a heated seat.

I often asked my Japanese friends why central heating, double glazing and insulation did not come as standard in Japan's extreme climate. The explanations I received were inconclusive. I was told that stagnant air is the greatest enemy of the Japanese home, thus houses are designed to be as draughty as possible to deter mould. Whilst it may help keep fungi at bay during the humid summer months, it means that winters are exceptionally cold in the Japanese home.

***

The massive snow falls that Fukui received had a dual effect on accessibility. On the one hand, they made hundreds of miles of pavements and roads impassable, but on the other, the snow opened up thousands of acres of previously inaccessible land.

You see, Fukui, and indeed many parts of rural Japan, is covered in rice paddies. In fact, if a piece of land is not a mountain or covered with a building, it's probably a rice paddy. Rice paddies give the impression of countryside and nature, especially during the harvest season when they become a bright green sea of rice that ripples and dances in the breeze. But there is a certain deception to this scene; rice paddies are very much of the 'look but don't touch' type of nature. They are not a place where you can throw down a rug and have a picnic, or kick a football about. They are strictly off limits and provide no use for recreation.

My little town of Ono, 'the big field', was known for its paddies. However, though my apartment was surrounded by great swathes of greenery, I could not enter this world. I often longed to immerse myself in nature, but I was largely confined to the tarmac roads and pavements. Unlike the rolling hills of England, grass is not a common feature of the Japanese landscape; there were almost no lawns, no pastures or parks in Ono, and sports pitches were made of gravel or sand. Because of this, I sometimes felt a little hemmed in by my surroundings and missed being able to roam across the green and pleasant fields like I had done back home.

But the winters of Fukui altered this balance; the snow blocked roads, cut off railways and prevented pavement access, but opened up the huge expanse of rice paddies, creating one massive footpath to anyone with a pair of snow shoes.

I snow-shoed around the beautiful wooden shrines that perfectly complemented the natural scenery, past miniature statues of Buddha dressed in red winter hats and scarves, and through the straight, bright green, bamboo groves, a particularly surreal scene, bamboo being a plant that is associated with hot, tropical weather. It was on days like these that I felt that happiness could be inhaled, simply by breathing the cool, crisp air.

That winter I began an intense affair with *yuki*, a truly cold-hearted lover, around which my life completely revolved. If I wasn't snowboarding in it, I was driving my Suzuki Wagon in it. If I wasn't walking the school dog in it, I was cross-country skiing in it. If I wasn't snow-shoeing around ancient wooden temples in it, then I was sitting at my desk, mesmerised by it falling from the ominous clouds above. If I wasn't shovelling it, I was thinking about it, and if I was doing none of the above, I was probably dreaming about it.

When I first arrived in Fukui on that sweaty, August summer day, it was hard to see how a snow lover could ever find satisfaction here. But after that record-breaking winter, one of the heaviest in recent history, I could only say *domo arigatou gozaimasu* (thank you very much) to the Japanese snow gods for showing me the deepest, most incredible snow that I'm ever likely to have the pleasure of experiencing.

Chapter 11
Feeling Foreign In Fukui

The Japanese are generally considered by the outside world to be a polite and peaceful people. Indeed, this is the impression I got from living amongst them. But of course, just like any population of any country on earth, there are those who don't adhere to our neatly packaged stereotypes. It was my friend 'Will Spin' – fellow English teacher and aspiring DJ – who was to draw out violence in a Japanese person that is rarely seen.

Will was enjoying the growing success that a foreign DJ can expect in small-town Japan. Although the country is renowned for being a difficult place for foreigners to find acceptance, there are advantages to being an outsider too. During the *sakoku* – which means 'closed country' – period, no foreigner could enter Japan, nor could any Japanese leave, under the penalty of death. For over two hundred years, Japan locked itself away from the world, imposing this state of isolation and only allowing limited trade with the Chinese and Dutch. It was not until 1853, when Commodore Matthew Perry of the US Navy forced Japan to open its doors through the threat of attack with technologically superior firepower, that *sakoku* finally came to an end.

Foreigners still find it hard to penetrate deep into Japan's complicated culture, but in this case, Will's *gaijin* status was an asset. As a dedicated drum and bass music aficionado who was from the UK – the birthplace of this dance music genre – Will came hardwired with credibility, which opened doors that might have remained closed to natives. A form of positive discrimination, it plays on the Japanese fascination with many things Western.

Will practised his DJing constantly. When not working, he could usually be found in his bedroom, splicing together the latest tracks on his record decks. He was dedicated to his art and worked tirelessly to further his DJ career. He played regular gigs at Fukui night spots, often accompanied by Mitch, a well-muscled and somewhat mysterious member of the ex-pat community, who took to the mic and jabbered freestyle lyrics over Will's tracks. Will also appeared on local radio and schmoozed with music industry types – at least, schmoozed as much as you could in a rural Japanese backwater.

I was a big fan of Will's shows and had danced the night away on several occasions in the sweaty, coin-sized clubs of Fukui city. Unfortunately, Will's middle-aged Japanese neighbour apparently wasn't a big drum and bass fan, and this is what led to the attack.

One day, Will was happily bouncing around his bedroom practising his latest set when he heard heavy banging at his front door. Before he could answer, the door burst open and in stormed the neighbour, a large man, even by Western standards. Will's incessant basslines, which easily penetrated the thin walls of the apartment building, had finally driven the man into a mission to silence the budding DJ.

'When he didn't take off his shoes at the door, I knew there was going to be trouble,' Will had told me.

Indeed, it is a massive no-no in Japan to walk into someone's home without first removing your shoes. Upon realising the seriousness of the situation and fearing trouble, Will immediately apologised and offered to turn the music down. Either the message was misunderstood or it was simply too little, too late. The home invader launched himself at the source of the musical misery – Will's record decks – attempting to tear them from the table top, hurl them to the ground and put a stop to the pounding basslines once and for all.

Now, Will was almost certainly in the wrong. He admitted that he probably did play his music a little too loudly, and the fact that his neighbour worked nightshifts and had to sleep during the day didn't help matters. But Will wasn't about to let his beloved set of record decks go down without a fight. Rather than letting the neighbour destroy his valuable equipment, he clung tightly to the decks, wrestling them away from the attacker and preventing them from being thrown to the floor.

Realising that he wasn't going to be able to neutralise the weapons of sound so easily, the attacker switched targets and went to work on Will himself, unloading a series of kicks and punches to Will's head and torso. With adrenaline coursing, a brawl ensued. Will attempted to block the onslaught and eject the man from his house.

'I was really frightened. I didn't know how it was going to end; how far was this guy going to go before he was satisfied?'

After a stream of Japanese abuse, a barrage of punches and much blocking and parrying, Will finally succeeded in bundling the attacker out of the front door, where he deposited a final kick to Will's groin as he exited. In total shock and fearful of what might happen next, Will slammed the door, locked it and called his boss, who phoned the police.

They turned up shortly after but were unhelpful and rather blasé about the whole thing. It seemed they sided with invader and after a frustrating few hours, Will decided it wasn't worth pressing charges. He did however keep the volume down ever after.

This was the most violent incident that I ever heard of from a Japanese person towards a foreigner in Fukui, but sometimes the locals displayed their disapproval of *gaijin* in other ways.

Brandon, my American friend and fellow snow-lover, had an incredible passion for learning the local lingo. He studied and practised Japanese voraciously, which enabled him to have a high level of communication with the natives. One of the ways in which he put this to use was in the acquisition of Japanese ladies.

In the land of the love hotel, Western males are seemingly highly prized accessories and most find that compared to their native lands, getting attention from the opposite sex is remarkably easy. Now, as I was very happy with my English girlfriend, I can only speak from what I saw and heard, but it's a well documented and oft discussed phenomenon amongst the ex-pat community in Japan that Western males are granted enhanced powers of attraction as soon as they pass through immigration.

This *'gaijin* pulling power' has been perfectly illustrated in a comic strip called 'Charisma Man' that was created in the late 1990s by two Canadians, Larry Rodney and Glen Schroeder. The story features a young, spotty man, who works in a fast food joint. In his native Canada he is regarded as a nerd and girls shun him. But one day he leaves Canada and travels to Japan. As soon as he touches down, this scrawny geek is redrawn as a square-jawed hunk who has beautiful Japanese girls falling at his feet.

Our hero has become 'Charisma Man' and his newly found superpowers enable him to attract hordes of pretty Japanese girls. He has only one weakness: 'Western Woman'. Like Kryptonite is to Superman, Western Woman is to Charisma Man. When she appears in the frame, his good looks and charm vanish, and he is reduced to the spotty dweeb that he really is.

Though exaggerated, there is truth in the character of Charisma Man. Japan does have a reputation for attracting slightly geeky, social misfits who while not exactly fighting off the females in their home countries, manage to punch well above their weight in Japan.

Indeed, Western men seem to be viewed as a unanimously high quality species by some Japanese females. Known for their chivalry and their generously-sized manhood, they are reputed for 'treating the ladies right'. There are even Japanese magazines and websites offering advice on how to ensnare a Western man.

Brandon however, didn't fit the geek profile and being able to speak a good level of Japanese made him even hotter property in the eyes of the local ladies. He was only too happy to oblige their inquisitive nature, dating a string of Japanese girls before settling on a longer term relationship. But not everyone approved of such behaviour.

It was a Monday morning when Brandon walked into the staffroom of the rural school where he worked and was immediately summoned to the headmaster's office. They had received a serious complaint from an elderly Fukui woman. A Western male fitting Brandon's description had committed an unthinkable act. He had been spotted holding hands. With a Japanese girl.

Brandon was completely unsure of what to say. Back home in America, he had been a serial hand-holder where the practice is still legal. As far as he knew, it was not an offence to hold hands with a girl in Japan. But then this was Fukui, a land left behind in many aspects of modernisation. Who knew what local by-law on mixed-race palm-to-palm contact existed here?

Brandon decided to come clean. Yes, he had been on a date with a Japanese girl on the day in question – but that was his private business and since when had it been a crime to hold hands with a girl?

The school conveyed that they had no specific objection to him making hand-on-hand connections with native ladies, but as they had received a formal complaint they were obliged to follow it up. The matter was then passed higher to the Fukui Board of Education, who also questioned Brandon. After some discussion, no further action was taken. It was eventually agreed that holding hands with a girl was not an offence, even in Fukui.

It later transpired that other male English teachers in the area had also been called in for questioning. Nothing more was ever uncovered about the old woman. All we know is that she found the idea of a Western man holding hands with a Japanese woman so upsetting that she went to a lot of trouble to track down the culprit.

I suggested that Brandon might use the 'handshake loophole' defence, if ever caught again.

***

Unlike Will and Brandon, I personally never experienced any form of attack or verbal disapproval from anyone in Japan. On the contrary, I found the local population to be the friendliest, most generous and kind people I have ever had the pleasure of living amongst. But after several months in Ono, certain aspects of life in small town Japan did begin to grate.

It was the blatant staring that really started to rile me. Whether at *Hachi Ban Ramen* – the local noodle bar – or shopping at *Mitsua* supermarket, I always felt like I was being watched and talked about. People would point and whisper, as if they had never seen such a strange creature before. When I had first arrived in Ono, I had almost enjoyed this attention. The fact that I was worthy of a second look simply for not being Japanese was quite amusing but as the months passed, all the novelties of life in Japan began to wear off.

Going to the supermarket wasn't the wondrous experience that it had been when I first arrived. The indecipherable instructions on the back of food packets, which were once exotic had long since been decoded. For me, Ono had become home. But for the locals, the nature of my foreignness was a novelty that would never wear off.

I entered a period where I no longer wanted to go out in public. I became slightly withdrawn. I longed to be able to shop at the local supermarket or sit in a restaurant in peace, without being stared at or whispered about. But this rarely happened. My very presence would cause heads to turn, track and lock. Slack-jawed and bug-eyed, there was no attempt at a subtle glance, just blatant stares or even worse: 'the nudge'.

'*Gaijin*! Look! Over there, a *gaijin*! Quick quick! Look at him!'

All ages were guilty, but the worst offenders were *obaasans* – elderly Japanese women. I found myself resenting these goggled-eyed grannies at times, a silent rage building up inside me.

'WHAT ARE YOU LOOKING AT? Ain't you never seen a white boy before?'

I accepted that Ono was a small town in rural Japan and that foreigners were, and still are, a rarity. Yet the JET programme had been sending westerners here for some 20 years. Why were we still such objects of curiosity?

Part of my frustration during this period was perhaps down to some form of 'culture shock'. We had all been warned about this before our arrival in Japan, in various lectures and manuals, but it had such a vague definition it was meaningless. Described as 'anxiety or feelings of surprise, disorientation, uncertainty and confusion', it seems you can blame pretty much any negative feeling on culture shock. Under this definition, most people experience culture shock every day, even in their own cultures. Had a bad day at work? Culture shock. Feeling ill? Culture shock. Girlfriend just dumped you? Culture shock. Shocked by the culture? Culture shock.

There are apparently three phases to Culture Shock. Phase 1 is the 'Honeymoon Phase', where everything is new, exciting and fascinating. Phase 2 is the 'Negotiation Phase' when feelings of excitement give away to frustration and anger; everything is difficult and even depressing. And Phase 3 is the 'Adjustment Phase', where things become more normal, and you accept both the positive and negative differences that exist between your home and adopted country and are able to feel comfortable. There is also 'Reverse culture shock', which happens upon your return and was something that I most definitely would suffer from later on.

But for the most part, I never really experienced any negative feelings associated with culture shock. I seemed to skip Phase 2 and spent my two years in a continuous state of excitement and fascination, whilst at the same time feeling comfortable in my surroundings. This brief period of annoyance with the locals' stares was the closest I got to the downside of living in rural Japan. Although I still maintain that being stared at and whispered about is downright rude and would be enough to piss anyone off in any country or culture. No matter how 'tall' your nose is, how blue your eyes are, or how blond your hair is (and my hair's not even very blond).

But during these frustrating times there was one place I could always rely on to relax: my local bar, *Yumeya*. Here I was treated just like anyone else. I could wander in, take a seat at the bar and chat with familiar faces. Yasu would tell me about the mountain he had just climbed, Long Piece would tell me of his tiring day breaking rocks, and Gennai would ask when I was going to introduce him to some foreign ladies.

So despite my occasional annoyance at Ono's voyeurs, I conceded that if being stared at on a regular basis was the only price to pay, then I was happy to cough up. Life was full of adventure, the job was easy and aside from the dreaded 2-1 class, enjoyable. It paid well enough, meaning money was never a concern and with all of Ono's outdoor allure, I was content to allow myself to be a talking point amongst the locals in return for days that were certainly never boring.

And when it did all get a little too much, Yasu's *sake* and home-smoked cheese would always set the world to right.

Chapter 12
Holy Snow on Hakusan

Brandon is not a happy man. He's physically exhausted and is having difficulty breathing. He is verbally abusing the mountain, claiming the situation to be 'ridiculous' among other, less flattering terms.

I'm not faring much better. I've just lost my footing and am sliding down a steep slope at alarming speed, clinging to my snowboard with my left hand and desperately trying to halt my descent with my right. It's times like this that I wonder why I chose a snowboard over skis. Our Japanese friends, Yasu, Yomei and Adachi (who are all of the two-plank discipline), have made short work of the steep traverse. They are now sitting in sun, patiently waiting for the two snowboarding foreigners to play catch up.

We were twenty-five hundred metres up into Japanese airspace on *Hakusan*, an extinct volcano. Situated on the main island of Honshu, the mountain spans the prefectures of Fukui, Ishikawa and Gifu, and is one of the *nihon sanmeizan*: Japan's three most sacred mountains. As a result, many people come to the mountain each year on a *Shinto* pilgrimage, though most come to pray to the spirit of the mountain, rather than the spirit of the snow.

Even though the last lifts of Fukui's ski areas closed weeks ago, snow still sat on the shoulders of the mountains. Under the guidance of our bar owner and mountaineering friend Yasu, we were now embarking on our third, and most adventurous backcountry snow climb so far.

It's been a long, tiring hike, and there's more to come. We started early this morning, taking a suspension bridge over a fast flowing river, then hiking up a stream bed before hitting a narrow, rocky path that wound its way up through wooded slopes. The hot spring sun beats down on us, and the snowboard, water, food and clothes that we carry on our backs make a heavy burden.

After two hours of walking up a stone and rock path, we reach the ragged edge of the snowline. Here we stop for a welcome rest; my legs are already feeling the exertion. I gulp down some *Pocari Sweat* and nibble on strips of breaded horse *kastu*. We exchange greetings with another group of climbers who pass as we sit in the shade of dwarfed paper birch trees.

'*Tabete kudasai*! (Please eat!)' shouts Yasu, as he cooks up a local delicacy called '*ton chan*' (cow intestines), on his camp stove. It's not exactly gourmet, but the chewy tissue goes down well after burning so many calories on the way up.

As we move further up the snowline, the difficulty of the hike increases. The spring snow is so compact that Yasu advised us to leave our snowshoes in the car. He's right – they were an unnecessary weight but, without them, the soles of my old Merrel hiking shoes are now almost slick without grip, and I keep slipping and falling in the snow. Brandon too experiences similar problems, especially during some of the steepest sections, where he takes two steps forward, only to slide one step back. However, little by little, after several breaks and around four hours, we make vertical progress, eventually stopping at the top of a steep chute for lunch.

From there, we can see the peak, perhaps just thirty minutes away. Sitting in the sun, we each drink a can of *Kirin* beer to celebrate our progress. Yasu always brings a can of beer with him to toast the mountain when he reaches the top. Today he's decided to celebrate before we even get there. Perhaps it's a sign of confidence in his team. It's certainly a nice spot he's chosen; below are almost 200 square miles of the Hakusan national park. Down there, summer has almost arrived; up on the mountain it's still very much spring.

Hakusan is one of Japan's most popular mountains for climbing in summer and a large lodge sits just below the summit where climbers can stay overnight. Its climbing season is longer than Fuji's and though it's not the national icon that Fuji is, Yasu tells us it's a much better mountain to climb.

'The official climbing season has not yet begun, that's why there are so few other people about today,' he explains.

'It gets very busy in the summer, so I prefer to climb it when it's still cloaked in snow. And the ski down is much more fun than walking.'

From where we sit, we can see a shrine and a traditional red Japanese gate – a *torii*. Brandon and I discuss the idea of building a jump up to it and performing a few snowboarding tricks to impress our Japanese friends, but the idea is quickly dismissed as a waste of precious energy.

Yomei and Adachi, our climbing companions, are in their late twenties and both keen and talented skiers. We note that they only address Yasu by his surname, the respectful way. They tell us that Yasu is still considered a mountaineering legend in these parts. Brandon and I were later to quiz Yasu about this – had we been rude by referring to him via his first name? Apparently not; it's OK because we're foreign, and know no better.

After lunch comes the final assault: a quick blitz to take us to the top. Re-energised by cow intestines and horse meat and slightly light-headed from the beer and altitude, summit fever has set in. My pace picks up as I follow in the footsteps of Yasu, while he powers ahead to the peak.

Yasu, a smoker and self-confessed alcoholic, put us young, 'healthy' whipper-snappers to shame. But then he has conquered Himalayan peaks, whilst Mount Fuji is the highest that Brandon and I have ever climbed.

Yasu used to be a ticket collector for JR – Japan Rail – but his love for the mountains meant he sought a more flexible lifestyle. Owning a bar has given Yasu the freedom to climb and ski mountains, sometimes for days at a time, whenever the desire presents itself. Often, we would turn up at his bar ready for a night of drunken revelry, only to find the lights off and the door locked; Yasu was out climbing some remote peak again!

Our friendship quickly blossomed during the long winter nights through a mutual love of mountains, snow and music. With Yasu as a guide, we had got to know all the local hotspots in the Okuetsu Mountains as we followed him up densely forested slopes, onto open plateaus and down steep snowy chutes.

There is much rejoicing at having reached the top of Hakusan. Brandon in particular is especially happy and in true American fashion lets rip with a series of 'Whoops!' and 'Hell Yeahs!'. Little does he know what's in store for him on the way down.

We pause for a short while to take in the views of the valley, before swapping shoes for boards, donning gloves and beginning the descent. The first slope is pure joy; we cruise down the perfect pitch in the sunshine-sugar-snow, feasting on spectacular scenery and carving clean white lines into the surface of the speckled, rippled, dirt-ridden snow.

Yasu is leading the pack and going at quite a speed when he starts to wobble. He manages to keep upright for a few more metres before WHAM! – he hits the deck, leaving a ski and his poles strewn out in his wake. We follow at a more sensible speed, anxious for our leader, but after confirming that he is not seriously injured, we all have a good laugh and continue onwards, with Yasu tempering his pace from then on.

We soon reach a snow-less rocky outcrop that forces us to unstrap our boards and walk. This brings us to the top of another slope, steep and littered with rock and stone. We carefully make our way down the pitch, but are then faced with a long and challenging traverse to get to the next slope.

It's at times like this that I'm reminded of how impractical snowboards are. Whilst Brandon and I are continually unstrapping our boards, scrambling up, slipping down and generally struggling to make our way across this steep and awkward section, the skiers are far ahead, traversing the terrain with ease.

This is when Brandon decides he wants out. Physically exhausted, and having difficulty breathing, he is, to put it mildly, very unhappy.

However, we both know that the only way down, is across, so we continue the slow traverse, praying we won't take another fall, whilst our Japanese skiing friends wait patiently in the sun, and most probably have a good chuckle at our predicament.

Eventually, we make it over to where they are sat, but by this time Brandon is past the point of no return. All traces of his love for snow have long since evaporated.

'I want a chopper!' he gasps, and I believe he's serious but we're on our own, and he knows the air support will never come.

Next is the final straight, back down to whence we came. Yomei and Adachi, who are both talented freestyle skiers, fly down, popping 360 spins at every available opportunity. I attempt to follow suit but end up misjudging and having a close encounter with a tree.

The very last stretch is a battle through the forest. As the trunks close in around us, tight technical snowboarding is required to navigate through the birch and pine. Somewhere along the way we meet an out-of-control telemark skier. He doesn't appear to have grasped the most important element of skiing – how to stop – thus has a series of quite spectacular collisions with trees, rocks and other people, leaving him with a bloody nose.

By this time Brandon has given in to the mighty mountain and has fully accepted defeat. He removes his board and makes the remainder of his way down on foot. He is fuming and I wonder if, after this, he'll ever want to see a mountain again.

Eventually the trees become too dense to ride through at all, so boards and skis go back onto our backpacks, and out come the hiking poles. Yasu says his goodbyes and speeds off down the mountain; he must get back home to open his bar. This leaves the rest of us to make our way back at a more leisurely pace.

That final hike is the hardest of all. Exhausted from our long ascent, tricky traverses, heavy gear, and in dire need of decent rest, we still have almost two hours of walking to get back to base. With aching legs and shoulders, sore feet and bodies in need of some serious tender loving care, we *gaman* (soldier on). Finally, as we re-enter the valley and near our starting point, Brandon's spirits begin to rise. By the time we reach the cars he is back to his normal jovial self, and we are already laughing and joking about how he 'lost it' up there.

From top to bottom, the trip has taken us nine and a half hours. It has left us thoroughly exhausted and good for nothing but bed. We've paid our pilgrimage price to the mighty Hakusan in the form of kilojoules, sweat and American tears. Today was more about the hiking, scenery and camaraderie than the snowboarding but, despite our fatigue, it's been an incredible experience and a great work-out.

It appears that Yasu also had a good time. As I near my car, I notice something stuck under the wiper, flapping in the gentle breeze. On a scrap of paper is a hastily written message from our local legend. In scrawled Japanese *katakana* script it reads:

'Za Dogusu Dangurazu!'

A broad smile instantly spreads across my face. He means 'The Dog's Danglers!', a slang phrase for 'Awesome!' that I'd been bandying around his bar recently.

It seems all those nights spent 'internationalising' with Yasu over cups of *sake* are beginning to rub off on the locals.

Chapter 13
Tales of Tokyo

It was 5:30am when the bus ejected us into downtown Tokyo. Gritty-eyed and groggy from lack of sleep, I climbed down into the depot and sucked in diesel fumes. Tilly, an English rose, Laura, a fine Finnish girl whose English was so good she was teaching it, and a few other friends followed.

Having had unsavoury experiences on long distance buses in the past, I had been reluctant to decline the much speedier bullet train. But getting the overnight bus from Fukui had been much cheaper and the vehicle itself had surprised me, pleasantly. With seats that reclined to almost horizontal, it was the most comfortable coach I had ever ridden. It was, however, still just a coach, and didn't provide passengers with the deepest of sleep.

Exiting the fluorescent glow of Shinjuku bus station we stepped into Tokyo daylight and almost stumbled over a sleeping *salaryman*. Fully suited, he was passed out on the side of the street, his head laid upon his briefcase as he dozed. *Salarymen* sleeping in the public places of Japan's cities is no uncommon sight. You can play 'spot the sleeping *salaryman*' in most urban areas, but for a high score, check subway trains, station platforms and massage chairs of department stores.

Taking advantage of our imposed early waking, we wandered to the now famous Tsukiji Fish Market, which was in full swing. Said to be the biggest wholesale fish and seafood market in the world, it has become a major attraction for foreign visitors. Our sluggishness was quickly forced out of us; we had to stay alert to stay alive. Miniature trucks and propane-powered fork-lifts zipped along narrow aisles shifting their fishy cargo. One ill-considered step would lead to a collision.

Creatures from all parts of the deep were on sale: orange octopus, striped cuttlefish, eel floating in their own blood, *fugu* (puffer fish), flat fish, spider crabs, catfish and caviar. From seaweed to sea snails to sardines to squid, if it lives under the sea, you can probably buy it at Tsukiji. But of all the marine life, it is the mighty *maguro* – the tuna – which is most highly prized and it's the tuna auction that draws most visitors. Buyers inspected rows upon rows of torpedo shaped carcasses, each one a frosty white, marked with a number and some *kanji*. Then a little man standing on a stool rang a bell, and the bidding commenced. Auctioneers around the world have the ability to spout high-speed gobbledygook, which is completely unintelligible to everybody apart from the bidders. The tuna auctioneers of Tsukiji market were no different.

Once purchased, men came with little metal gaffs, swung their spikes into the frozen carcasses and dragged them away. All the fish guts and gore was far too much for Flick and Lewis, the two vegetarians of our group, who left within ten minutes. It was the tuna being cut into hunks with an electric band saw that finished them off. They retreated to a nearby restaurant; it sold *sushi*.

As I wandered in awe, snapping away with my camera, it occurred to me how the workers of Tsukiji must get very annoyed at all the annoying tourists. We get in the way, take photos of everything yet never buy anything. Indeed, Tsukiji has since become too popular for its own good. Due to the increasing numbers of tourists, Tsukiji has now restricted access, only allowing visits at certain times to certain areas. Reportedly, it's not just the volumes of visitors that have led to this but the 'bad manners' of many foreign tourists, who have violated hygiene rules and acceptable codes of conduct by touching the fish.

After taking our fill of fish photos, we reconvened and then headed onwards, deep into the dense concrete of Tokyo city.

***

The next stop on our Tokyo tour was the district of Harajuku. After months in rural Japan, where life had slowly become familiar, we had come to the capital to play at being tourists again, determined to see as many of the city's clichéd sights as we could.

Descending into Tokyo's underworld, we hopped aboard a subway train. As I seated myself next to two ladies dressed in colourful *yukata* (summer kimono), a very old man shuffled along the platform towards our carriage. The doors bleeped, indicating they were about to close, but the old man shuffled still closer. Now on the very edge of the platform he paused and extended his neck slightly to look inside the carriage. His projecting bald head gave him the air of an ancient tortoise, looking out of its shell. Then the doors closed, leaving his body on the platform and his head trapped inside. Two young men immediately jumped to his rescue, each taking a door and heaving it open.

'Are you OK?' they asked, steadying the poor chap. But he just mumbled something and didn't move. He seemed slightly stunned. Then the doors bleeped again. The whole carriage watched and waited but the old man stayed still and the doors kept bleeping. The young guys begged him to step aboard, but he didn't move. The doors closed and again his head was clamped by the black rubber seals a second time!

I battled hard to contain my giggles; though I'd like to blame this on the Japanese game shows I'd been watching, in truth I've always had a 'developed' sense of Schadenfreude. Again the two young guys prised open the doors, freeing the old fellow, and this time he grunted, turned and wandered off down the platform, perhaps deciding it was safer to take the bus instead.

***

We had come to Harajuku to see the strangely dressed teenagers. This phenomenon is known as 'Cos Play' – costume play – or, in other words, dressing up in bizarre outfits and showing yourself off. There were various styles on view but by far the most popular was the 'French maid/little Bo-Peep' look. Known as 'Lolita' (or often just 'Loli') it's characterised by Victorian styled hair bows or bonnets, a bell shaped dress, frilly petticoat, blouse, knee-high socks, chunky platform heels, frilly umbrellas and lots of lace. Lolita fashion comes in many flavours: classic, country, sweet, sailor, punk and more. There are many magazines and websites devoted to Lolita fashion and its popularity has spread well beyond Japan's shores.

Scores of teenagers, mostly female, milled around in their outfits whipping out the 'Vs' to appease the relentless attack by the happy snappers. (It appears to be illegal to pose for a photograph without displaying the 'peace sign V' in Japan, which makes it infuriatingly difficult to get a natural-looking shot.)

Many of the photographers were unsavoury looking middle-aged Western men. One girl who had gone for the 'blonde Lolita' was especially popular, but didn't seem to be relishing the attention. I watched her trying to avoid being captured on film by one particularly depraved looking man, even shouting '*sukebe*! (pervert!)' at him. However, he wasn't put off and persevered until she eventually gave in, granting him a clear shot.

Just round the corner from Harajuku's Lolita ladies lies the entrance to the Meiji shrine. One of Japan's most famous, it was built in honour of Emperor Meiji, who is credited with opening up and modernising Japan, enabling it to become one of the world's great superpowers. The Meiji *torii* (gate) towers over us, and we instantly escaped the frenzy of the city and entered a much calmer, tranquil world.

Woods shaded the path. I paused at a great wall of white *sake* barrels, six high and some thirty barrels wide. Each was splashed with elaborate *kanji* and colourful artwork. These *kazaridaru* (decoration barrels) symbolise the importance of *sake* in Shinto. Apparently drinking it helps people 'come closer to the gods', which is one way of putting it I suppose.

Sake brewers supply shrines for various religious festivals, and the Meiji shrine accepts donations from every *sake* maker in the country.

We continued up the path that wound through forest. The trees cooled the air as we walked deeper into the shrine complex itself. Japan's temples and shrines are beautiful buildings, there's no doubting that, but you must be careful when visiting them. The now well documented syndrome of temple overdose (known as 'O.T.-ing') is a common complaint of visitors to the Far East. The illness is caused by trying to visit too many temples in a short space of time, and is common in Japan as well as China, Cambodia and Thailand. The symptoms are fatigue, boredom, and a desire to never see another temple as long as you live (these symptoms normally pass after the patient has been removed from temple stimuli).

The World Health Organisation states an Recommended Daily Allowance of one temple per day and I managed to avoid the condition by viewing temples in moderation.

Next we headed onwards to Yoyogi park. One of the largest green spaces in Tokyo, it's the place to come on a Sunday when Tokyoites of every sect come out to play. There are dreadlocked Japanese Rastas grooving to Marley; circles of drummers; teams of high school girls practising dance routines; old ladies moving through sets of tai-chi moves; high-kicking capoeira artists and families picnicking. A punk band was playing an upbeat set, and further on we saw the Japanese Teddy Boys. With huge, grease-backed quiffs, they are now somewhat of a Yoyogi phenomenon. Every Sunday they come, dressed in tight leather jackets and winklepickers to spend the day jitterbugging to '50s' rock 'n' roll.

We then wandered deeper into this oasis of green, which is surrounded by high-rise buildings, soaking up the buzzing atmosphere as we went. A man spun a pair of nunchuks with incredible speed, blurring as he switched hands and lashing out with a practice strike. A skateboarding dog zipped along a path, to cheers of *'sugoi'* (amazing!)

and '*kawai*!' (cute!). It's even possible to hire dogs at Yoyogi (though not skateboards) if you don't have one of your own.

***

Coming from the relative countryside of Fukui, it was Tokyo's renowned nightlife that was perhaps the thing we country folk were most looking forward to. That and the range of foreign foods that I now realised I missed so much. I greedily devoured pizza, curry and Thai during our stay, making the most of meals that were hard to come by in Ono.

Later we wandered the narrow, neon lit streets of Shinjuku, turning down offers of girls from burly bouncers, and sampling some of the numerous small bars to be found in this district.

Despite ranking as one of the world's most expensive cities, with the help of some Japanese connections we found a two-hour *nomihodi* (all you can drink) for a mere £10. Later on that night, I was once again taken aback by the kindness and generosity of Japanese strangers.

Numerous times in Fukui I had found the locals to be kind and helpful. But I had often wondered whether this was more a trait of country folk rather than the Japanese in general; indeed in many countries, rural people are more accommodating towards visitors than their busier city cousins.

We had been wandering aimlessly for some time, searching in vain for a decent bar. Two young Japanese guys who looked as though they knew the area were approaching so we stopped them and asked if they could recommend somewhere. They had been out on the town themselves and were heading home but kindly offered to walk us to a bar they knew of. Upon arriving, they insisted on staying for a drink and we chatted in Japanese. We learned a little of their Tokyo lives, jobs, and hobbies, but when the night came to a close, despite our protests they insisted on paying for all our drinks and refused to accept any money from us even though they had also told us how hard up they were. It seemed that the kindness of Japanese strangers was indeed a nationwide trait.

Having had a taste of urban life, it was now time for us country bumpkins to say *sayonara* to the city and return once more to our rural Japanese homeland. Fukui was calling.

Chapter 14
Cooling Off in the Kuzuryu

The pleasant cool of spring was fading into the heavy heat of summer. The cicadas had begun their throbbing calls and the awful humidity of Honshu was beginning to force itself upon us.

There was only so much cooling power my one rattling fan could provide, and in the absence of air conditioning, my sweaty apartment was the last place I wanted to lounge. But the people of Ono were lucky. We had a secret weapon against the heat. We had the Kuzuryu River.

It was only a fifteen-minute drive to this magical place. Caitlin, my Vikingly blonde and blue-eyed American friend and I had agreed we needed to cool off after work, so it was now towards the Kuzuryu River that we were heading. Across town we drove, the flat paddies turning to pine forests as we climbed higher. The road gripped the mountainside above the Kuzuryu gorge, passed through a great red *torii* (gate) that spanned the tarmac, and then under a giant rusting water pipe.

At a tumbledown house that was being reclaimed by undergrowth, we turned off the main road. Crossing the railway line that brought single carriage trains from Ono and took them up to Izumi, we entered Kadohara village, a cluster of perhaps twenty little houses. Making a turn here and there, we navigated the tight maze of homes, curled around another paddy, passed a little graveyard, and came up against a great wall of bamboo forest through which a narrow lane led. It spat us out at one of the most picturesque places I've ever known.

Completely hidden from view and barely signposted, it was a secret known only to locals. Guidebooks made no mention of it, and why would they? Kuzuryu's real beauty was in its raw beauty and as I would later discover to my amazement, natural splendour alone is no guarantee of appreciation in Japan. So it was spared from crowds and commerce of any kind. There were no souvenir shops and no food stalls; there wasn't even a vending machine.

Smooth boulders and rock led to the blue-green waters of the river. It swirled and rushed, going from deep, slow pools, to shallow, chattering flows, then curling round a wall of white rock. A grassy meadow sat under red-trunked pines, whose flattened boughs offered shade. Steep cliffs, smothered in stunted trees, rose from the far bank. Above, thick forest on round mountains provided the perfect screen to hide the river from human eyes.

Caitlin and I donned our swimmers, picked our way across the sun-warmed boulders and dove into the Kuzuryu's waters. Despite the heat of the day, the river was cold enough to shock; once we'd adjusted to it, however, it was a heavenly place to bathe.

The reason why this spot was so special was its lack of concrete. Japan has spent enormous amounts of money and time confining its rivers and streams with the stuff. Though Japan's love of concrete is well publicised, I was astounded at how much of their natural terrain has been encased. It really is very rare to see a river without banks of sloping concrete and many of their mountains, too, have been trussed in great concrete lattices. The most outrageous use of concrete I ever saw, though, was during the *sakura hamami* – the viewing of the cherry blossom.

One of the most celebrated times of the year, it's during late spring that the cherry blossom front sweeps up the country from Kyushu to Hokkaido, and with it, one hundred thousand parties are thrown beneath the boughs. I had spent a lovely day in the neighbouring town of Katsuyama, picnicking under the petals. But there I had seen not one, but two cherry trees whose hollows had been filled with concrete. Japan is still a very beautiful place, but it must have been so much more beautiful before so much of it was caked over with concrete.

Caitlin and I swam until the sun slipped below the mountains and cast a cool shadow upon the water. It was to become a regular post-work refreshment session and a welcome relief from the sweaty classrooms in which we worked.

***

Have you ever wondered how much a life is worth? Well, it was here at the Kuzuryu that I was to discover the exact value, in yen.

I had come with a few friends to while away the day at the river and, as it was particularly hot, several other people were around. One group were cooking *yaki-soba* (fried noodles) on a flat metal pan on a barbecue under a tree. A man was fishing further upstream, while we lazed on the smooth boulders by the pool on the meander of the river, warming up in the sun following a dip.

A man sat on the far bank of the river, basking and swigging on a beer. His son, a small child of around ten was splashing in the shallows on our side, under the watchful eye of his mother. But growing increasingly brave, the young boy decided to swim across the river to join his dad on the other side. He started well, paddling doggy, but when he hit the deeper water he began to tire. The father, who appeared to be more than a little tipsy, saw that his son was struggling, and quickly slipped in to the water to assist.

The mother became anxious, calling out to her son, but the dad had almost reached his boy, so everything would soon be OK. Or so we thought. But the boy was now running low on energy and the dad, who had definitely had more than a few beers, began floundering himself, panicking as he tried to keep his son's head above water, but unable to bring him back to the bank.

We sat watching the scene unfold from the rocks. It looked like they were in trouble, and a few other Japanese had turned to watch too, but there was no urgency in the air and we wondered if we had misread the situation. Perhaps it was all part of some swimming training programme?

The mother's wails soon put paid to that idea. She began to frantically shout and scream. The boy looked petrified and was starting to splutter and it didn't look like World's Best Dad was going to be able to solve the situation on his own. I decided that I'd rather risk helping someone who might not need help, than watch someone drown, so I skipped into the shallows, swimming out then diving up and under the boy to support some of his weight and assist the dad, who now also seemed almost drained.

It was no spectacular 'Baywatch-style' rescue. Within a minute or two, we were back in the shallows. The mother grabbed her crying child whilst the dad simply collapsed onto me in an exhausted embrace which lasted for such a long time that I began to feel quite uncomfortable.

'Thank you! Thank you! Thank you!' he kept repeating.

'You're welcome. It's nothing. Are you OK?' I said.

'Thank you! Thank you!'

Eventually, he found his own strength and released me from his grip. After a few more 'thank yous', mum, dad and son (who was still weeping hard) picked their way back over the rocks to their camp.

Ten minutes later, the family returned. The boy was still weeping; he had obviously had quite a fright. The father bowed and holding out his hand said:

'Please – take this'.

He held a 10,000 yen note – about £50. I flatly refused to accept, but he kept on insisting, repeating perhaps the only word he knew in English: 'Thank you'. 10,000 yen for a minute's work would have been nice, but of course, it would not have been right. So I thanked him again, but refused it with a firm finality. The mother then explained that her son had just learned to swim, but it was his first time in a river. The cold water had shocked him, and once out of his depth he had began to panic. The father, who still smelled of beer, hadn't been much help. I was just glad we had read the situation right.

We lingered a little longer and, as the shadows arrived, said our farewells to the family, wished the young lad good luck with his swimming career and headed back to Ono town.

***

The 'Ono swimming hole', as it was known to our tiny expat community, became one of my most treasured places in Japan. I visited it frequently throughout the summer and autumn, and even in winter when it was blanketed in snow. It was such a calming place. Sometimes I would just go up there alone, hop from one rock to the next and get right out into the middle of the flow. There, I would lie on a boulder and absorb the day's heat, just listening to the gurgle and splash of the river on its way down from the mountains. The song of the river's rush completely filled my thoughts and all woes were swept away by the current.

I was so taken by this little paradise that I decided to organise a little camp-out party. I picked a weekend and put out the word; bring your tent, some *sake* and your swimmers.

About thirty of Fukui's locals and expats arrived slowly throughout the day; all were wowed by the place. We pitched our tents under the shade of the pines, placed our cans of *Kirin* and *Chu-hi* in the stream that flowed from the forest into the river, and donned our trunks.

The day rolled on, hot and humid, making the cool waters of the Kuzuryu all the more alluring. A constant cycle of swimming, eating and drinking repeated itself.

I had invited some of my Japanese footballing friends along. A few months before, one night at my favourite bar Yumeya, I had announced that I wanted to play some football, a sport I've always enjoyed. Gennai – the loveable bar clown – had immediately made a call and arranged for me to join a local mixed team. It was a casual affair – at least as casual as any Japanese club or team can be – and was another ideal opportunity to meet more of the locals and practise my Japanese, as well as my ball skills.

Three of the team had come along. There was Junko, a pretty girl with high cheek bones and feline eyes who worked at the post office; Miki, long-lashed and petite with quite a case of *yaeba* (double tooth), she sold beauty products at Ono's shopping centre, and Yoshi, a twenty-something lad who worked in a pharmaceutical factory in the neighbouring town, Katsuyama.

Yoshi had an immaculately coiffured bouffant, even more coiffured than beauty-mad Miki's. Indeed there were two things that Yoshi loved more than anything else in this world: his car and his hair. He lavished all of his time and money on both. He was extremely protective of his highly styled mullet and refused to let anyone, or anything, touch it. At football, he never headed the ball and any attempt to touch his locks were met with serious rebuff.

But Yoshi's car was even more precious. I had once been permitted to travel in it, but only after Yoshi had made me place elasticated plastic coverings over my shoes first, the type that forensic scientists wear at crime scenes.

The car was cuboidal in shape and had blacked-out windows, an ultramarine lighting rig on the front, a super sub-woofer stereo and a mysterious black box built into the boot. This was locked, and despite me asking repeatedly what it held, he would only reveal that it was his 'secret box'. I had become good friends with Yoshi, and we often drank a beer after football. When he had discovered my love for *takoyaki* – fried octopus balls – he had even taken me to his cousin's *takoyaki* shop where I had got twelve *takoyaki* for the price of six.

Dusk approached and I lit the fire. It crackled and danced, drawing us in like moths. It was a perfect evening: an exquisite backdrop, an interestingly international collection of people and a few beers to help bring us all together. But there was something lurking in the undergrowth that we hadn't banked on.

Though bears roamed these parts, they had since returned to the forests and hadn't troubled the Ono folk since last autumn. No, our little party was to be disrupted by a far smaller foe. We knew that mosquitoes were rife, but no one had ever heard of the *buyo*. After that weekend, no one would ever forget about the *buyo*. It is translated as 'gnat' but it's like no gnat I've seen. A horrible little fly it draws blood when it bites. They arrived in their hundreds to plague us and we were ill-equipped to defend against them. Wearing just T-shirts and shorts, we provided a huge landing zone for them, and they drank their fill of blood. As the sun passed below the mountains and the light faded away, so did the *buyo*, much to our relief – though if we'd known the torment we'd be in for the next seven days, we would have been less relieved.

But we weren't to know that then and, with the swarms gone, the party continued into the night. The cycling whirr of the cicada and the chirp of crickets created the exotic feel of a tropical night. The flames ducked and weaved as we cooked chicken, juicy prawns and sweet potatoes over the fire.

It's a mathematical certainty that Boys + Girls + Booze + Water = Nakedness, so it wasn't long before bikinis and trunks were removed, and a good old fashioned skinny dipping session was in full swing. I swam out to a large boulder whose shoulders poked above the surface, and clambered atop, diving deep into the cool, black water, calmly holding my breath and swimming submarine before surfacing again in the lunar-lit ripples.

Despite repeated invitations, Junko, Miki and Yoshi could not be tempted to shed their clothes, or even enter the water at all. I later found out that the girls couldn't swim and Yoshi didn't want to mess up his mullet. So instead, my Japanese friends watched starlit bums and boobs bob up and down from the safety of the rocks. Afterwards, we regrouped at the fire to stare at the embers and drink into the night, before people began to peel off and retire to their tents.

Daylight came early, and as I am unable to sleep without perfect darkness, I was up and out of my tent at sunrise. The air was pleasantly cool, the grass dewy underfoot. I relit the fire and boiled water for tea. Slowly, people began to emerge, somewhat subdued. The day was spent lazing on the hot rocks and swimming again, as people slowly packed up and headed off to their respective parts of the prefecture.

Everyone agreed it had been a superb weekend, but we were all rather itchy. The bites of the *buyo* had swollen overnight. Sarah, a feisty young New Jersey girl, had been bitten on the upper lip, and it had swollen so much it looked as though she'd been in a fist fight (which I wouldn't have put past her!). Shannon, a petite Vancouverite, had several bites on her ankle and it was now so inflamed that she was unable to get her shoe on.

We all spent the following week scratching like crazy at the infuriatingly itchy bites and vowed to take ample supplies of insecticide next time.

***

Summer was rolling on, the holidays coming up fast. I would soon take to the high seas to join a fishing boat crew in a tiny town that would become, for a few months at least, the most famous in Fukui.

But before that, I had a meeting with 'the sock smeller'.

Chapter 15
The Sock Smeller

It was July 8th 2005, the day after the London bombings that had killed 56 and injured 700. I had arrived at work that morning to be summoned to the headmaster's office. A local newspaper wanted a comment from a real, live Englishman, and seeing as I was the only one in Ono, I got the job.

I had been in Yasu's bar the night before when I'd seen the news. I had watched scenes of a smouldering double-decker bus ripped open like a sardine tin with a growing sense of unease. It had been horrible to have the realisation that something awful had happened in my home country but not able to fully understand the rapid-fire report. My quote appeared in the paper the following day.

I was no stranger to the headmaster's office. Following our fishing trip last year, he had invited me in one afternoon to teach me the craft of carving *taketonbo*. Translating as 'bamboo dragonfly' – *taketonbo* look nothing like dragonflies. They are a traditional children's toy, consisting of a propeller on a stick and a more appropriate name would be 'bamboo helicopter'. You place the stick between your palms and spin it; the stick then launches the propeller blade sky high.

The headmaster was a master of carving *taketonbo* and had been keen to share his art with me. We drunk cold *oolong* tea as he explained the process and demonstrated how to shape the propeller. We had bonded further when he discovered that, just like him, I was *hidari te* (left-handed). I spent an enjoyable afternoon whittling away slithers of bamboo under his guidance and, by the end of his master class, I had shaped a crude, but functioning, *taketonbo*. We had gone outside for the test flight. Careful to avoid the *koi* pond and the manicured tress, I had spun my *taketonbo* stick, successfully launching my propeller into the air. It passed the test, though perhaps not with flying colours. So that I would have an example of a perfected model, the Headmaster gave me a *taketonbo* from his own personal collection, which he signed and dated.

It became one of my little treasures that I kept and still have to this day.

***

At 12:45 the lunchtime bell sounded. Meals were prepared by adult staff but it was the job of the students to serve it up. They donned white face masks and hats, wheeled in the food trolley and doled it out to their classmates. I admired the way students were taught to do things for themselves right from elementary school and learned to take on responsibilities from an early age.

Unlike school canteens in the UK, in Japan's rural schools, there was no choice on the menu; you simply ate what you were given. Today, the line up was:

1 x bowl of white rice
1 x bag of small dried whole fish
1 x boiled *daikon* stew
1 x lump of pineapple
1 x bottle of warm milk

Students were forbidden to bring in any food or sweets, so they tended to eat very healthily in school and were taught the importance of a balanced diet rather than gorging themselves on junk food every day. Indeed, there are far fewer obese people in Japan than in the UK, and the Japanese rank as the world's longest-lived people.

Wasting food was considered very bad form and I never saw any students or teachers leave as much as a single grain of rice. I'm not a fussy eater so normally ate whatever I was served, which on the whole was quite palatable. But occasionally, when I just couldn't stomach the rubbery squid, or the boiled *daikon*, I would mount an undercover food disposal mission. Today was one of those days.

I had developed a method that allowed me to get rid of disagreeable food without detection. As there was no canteen, I ate at my desk in the staff room. My desk had a wide drawer under it and I would place a piece of paper in the drawer and leave it slightly open. After a quick scan of the room to make sure nobody was looking, I would discreetly drop any offensive fodder into the drawer and onto the paper. At the end of the meal, I would fold up the paper, encapsulating the food and close the drawer. Later in the day I would dispose of the paper parcel, destroying all evidence and meaning that I didn't disgrace myself by playing the wasteful Westerner.

But today I had a close shave. I had almost been spotted by part-time, trainee teacher Ricki. Just as I was going for the drop, I realised Ricki was watching me, so I turned it into a fumble, cursing my chopsticks for extra authenticity.

Now, Ricki was a nice guy, but he was without doubt a little odd. Not just because he insisted that everyone (including the students) called him by his self-imposed nickname, which he had adopted from an American wrestler because it was a 'strong name with high power'. Not just because he was obsessed with moths and kept chrysalises in glass tanks. No, Ricki's oddness ran deeper than this, as I was soon to discover.

Ricki had befriended me shortly after our first meeting; his English was fantastic and he was overjoyed to have someone to use it on. In fact, Ricki's English was almost too good. So eager was Ricki to impress with his English-speaking ability, he would ensure our conversations were peppered with complex sentence constructions, unusual idioms and bizarre figures of speech. The problem was that it often took Ricki a little while to compose his lines, meaning that conversation could become laboured. He would insist I wait for him to regurgitate his latest learned catchphrase, even though I had understood his point three sentences back.

'I don't want to rain on your parade but the early bird is always catching the worm.'

'Don't you think it could be the red herring?'

'Let's just go back to the drawing board because there's no need to act like a bull in a china shop.'

Ricki also had a very unusual hobby. One night over a few beers, he had announced in a serious tone that one of his favourite pastimes was smelling his own socks. Now, if this happened to be a hobby of mine (it isn't), I would definitely keep it to myself. Ricki, however, proudly explained:

'Sam *san*, I love to smell my own socks. Every night before I go to bed, I take off my socks, put them on my face, and just smell them for ten minutes.'

'Do you like the smell of other people's socks, or just your own?' I asked.

'I could handle your socks also,' Ricki replied with complete sincerity.

I didn't have much more to say on the hobby of sock-smelling and I wasn't planning on lending Ricki my socks, so the conversation ended rather abruptly. However, Ricki's increasing strangeness didn't.

Ricki's English skills were so good that he could have used them to take him places – a translator or interpreter perhaps – but his social skills were less pronounced. He was somewhat of a loner at work, a square peg that didn't fit neatly into the round hole of Japanese society. He was always getting scowled at and scolded by our colleagues. They hammered him down, trying to make him fit, but he just began to splinter. And once that happened, nobody wanted to talk to him anymore. For this reason, Ricki was largely excluded from the staffroom chit-chat, sometimes left uninvited to *enkai*. They seemed to be well aware of his oddities and generally steered clear, which is why I think he valued our friendship so much.

When the annual school talent show came round, Ricki had asked if I would perform with him. I would play the drums while he sang some songs by the Japanese rock band 'Spitz'. I agreed and for a couple of weeks we practised our set after school. Ricki took it very seriously, coiffeuring his hair and donning a pair of aviator sunglasses, a tight T-shirt and a gold necklace to complete the rock-star look – even during rehearsals. But when it came to the big day, it was a total disaster. The PA system was too quiet and we couldn't hear the backing track properly. We went completely out of time, resulting in an awful cacophony in front of the whole school. I was desperate to call it off but Ricki insisted that the show must go on. It was a truly terrible performance and the most embarrassing fifteen minutes of my time in Japan. The audience clapped out of politeness but I knew it had been dire. Afterwards, Ricki was summoned to the headmaster's office and chastised for the bad show and because we had played for too long.

***

Ricki's oddest moment came a few weeks later at an *enkai* that he *had* been invited to. I was sitting at the low table chomping on fried chicken as Ricki explained his love for betting on the horses. The subject then moved on to music, sport, work and his university years. Eventually the topic of girls surfaced and he asked me what I looked for in a lady. He himself admitted he was very picky.

'They must be Japanese. I like Western women's curves, but I don't like their noses – too big.'

'They must have long hair and it must be black. Short or dyed hair is simply out of the question. And they must have a nice body.'

He proudly informed me that during his college years he had slept with ten women from across the country – *Hokkaidoites* to *Okinawans* – and never stayed with any of them for longer than a month. All very interesting, I thought to myself, though I was somewhat surprised to hear my colleague volunteer so much personal information, especially while completely sober. However, things started to turn heavy when he confessed that he could never fall in love with a woman.

'I only want them for their body,' he explained.

'I will never marry. I will never have children.'

At the grand age of 24, I thought it was a little early to rule this out, but Ricki continued:

'I have nothing to say to women. I am too shy and nervous in front of them. In fact, I prefer younger women.'

'How much younger?' I asked.

'Younger than me,' he replied.

'In fact, quite a lot younger.'

I tried to hide my shock by acting as though it was perfectly normal to announce such things at the dinner table but inside I felt very uncomfortable and quickly moved the conversation on to more wholesome topics.

***

Ricki was very loyal and would always report the staffroom gossip to me. He once even told me I was his mentor. He would come to me with his problems and ask me for advice. I occasionally invited him to join me and other friends for food or drink and he was always overjoyed to be at any gathering with foreigners. In this environment, he became animated and uninhibited, seemingly much more comfortable with English speakers than his own kind. But Ricki's inherent oddness and admission of his unsavoury tendencies for younger girls meant that after his short contract at my school ended, I rarely saw him again. Ricki's farewell note to me read:

Dear Sam,

I've got to go now. I appreciate all the help that you've given me. Thank you for everything you did. I always remember you. I'll get in touch with you if things let up a bit. Last but not least, I'm always on your side. I wish you all the best.

Ricki

Ps You can touch base with me at anytime. So if you can, count me in at your social gatherings.

I never did touch base with Ricki again. I hope he has fared well, but can't help feeling that he was destined for a difficult life.

Chapter 16
Adrift on Obama Bay

It's 3am when the alarm goes off.

'Time to go fishing,' says Ryan.

I'm tired, I'm grumpy and it's dark outside. Why had I been so keen to get up at stupid-o-clock to join the crew of a fishing boat? When the idea had been raised over beers a few days ago, it had all seemed like great fun. Now the prospect of having to leave a warm futon and take to the high seas in the dead of night is far less appealing.

I had come to the bay town of Obama to visit my friend Ryan. Despite hailing from landlocked Tennessee, Ryan had the accent and attitude of a Californian surf dude. If the people of Ono were Fukui's mountain folk, then the natives of Obama were the beach bums of the prefecture. Ryan's appetite for adventure and apparent lack of concern for his own safety instantly appealed to me and time spent with him would inevitably end in some sort of escapade. Obama, which means 'little beach', suited Ryan well. Down in Fukui's sleepy south, it had the same easy, breezy outlook on life that he did: never rushed, ever up for a good time.

Ryan's outgoing nature had led him to befriend his neighbour Jerry, a fisherman. For no reason other than it was a new experience, Ryan had asked if he could join Jerry and his crew on their boat one day. No doubt bemused, Jerry had agreed, and Ryan had been chugging out to sea in the very small hours for the last few weeks, before heading to the local school where he taught English. As soon as Ryan had told me about Jerry and his fishing expeditions, I had wanted a piece of the action. But in the cold hours of pre-dawn, as I sat at the table of Ryan's trailer-park home supping on coffee, I struggled to stop myself crawling back to my *futon*.

***

Fifteen minutes later the caffeine has kicked in and I'm sitting in the back of Jerry's car, chatting away. An incredibly friendly and interesting man, Jerry's life story could fill many pages of this book.

A fifty-something Filipino, he had lived in Japan for eight years after being smuggled through China and Korea. Unknowingly used as a drug mule, he had lived in hovels packed full of other illegal immigrants and had been trapped into slave labour by his smugglers. He eventually escaped and had found his way to Obama, where he had a friend. Now married to a Japanese woman and fully legal, Jerry makes his simple living as a fisherman, pulling in his nets as the sun rises each morning.

It's still dark when we arrive at the tiny harbour to discover it has been a disastrous night. They are two crew down; one man's father had passed away in the night, and in a completely unrelated incident, another's house had burnt down! Despite being mere landlubbers, it seemed that our extra hands on deck would be welcomed.

After some hushed greetings and bows, we step aboard one of their two boats. It's a small vessel with just a tiny open wheelhouse and a few wooden chests secured to the deck. At one time everything had been blue but now dark wood was showing through, the paint having peeled over the years. Jerry hands me a pair of rubber boots, some rubber gloves and a pair of rubber overalls. '*Arigatou gozaimasu*' I thank, as I jiggle into them and fasten the buckles. With the crew all aboard, the diesel engine gurgles to life and we chug out into the bay's inky waters. One man takes the chunky wooden tiller and points our prow seaward, whilst another, brown and lined from being washed in salt and sun all his life, curls up on a chest to sleep. The second boat follows in our wake.

Obama Bay is a bay within a bay. Situated at the tail end of Fukui's comma-shaped prefecture is the large bay of Wakasa, sheltered somewhat by the inward curl of the coast. Obama Bay lies inside Wakasa's and is further protected by two spits of land that project either side like the mandibles of a stag beetle, so its waters are usually calm, just as they were now.

Ryan and I sit on a vacant chest, lit by the halogen glow of the deck light. The boat rises and falls gently as small waves meet us. It's still dark but ahead, out through the mouth of the bay, the horizon is just beginning to hint at a new day. Aside from the glug-glug-glug of the engine, all is quiet and little is said. The rock of the boat is soporific but the cool sea air keeps me wakeful. We chug on, around a small headland and through the bay's jaws, out into the open water of Wakasa. The boat pitches a little more as a bigger swell rocks us.

A cigarette dangles from our pilot's mouth. An old man of the sea, his face is thin and weathered, almost skeletal, and he wears a black baseball cap. He pushes the tiller away, changing our course slightly and we sail further away from land. I can just make out the dim lights in the distance that mark the town of Obama behind us. Ahead, there was nothing but open ocean until the Korean peninsula 400 miles away.

We chug on for a while longer, eventually reaching a group of buoys. Here, the pilot cuts the throttle and for a few moments all is silent. We glide towards the line of yellow floats as he manoeuvres the boat expertly, bringing it alongside these markers, below which elaborate mazes of nets hang down into the deep.

It's time to start work. The man who has slept all the way rises from his hard bed, takes a long pole and hooks a rope from the water, which is attached to the net. He pulls it in, then shows me how to feed it into a small, somewhat antique-looking electric winch, gesturing caution at its plastic teeth.

'*Kiotsukete ne* (be careful)' he says, making it clear that the winch will happily eat my fingers if given the chance.

With all the care he advises, I help the net slowly rise from the deep, water draining away as it leaves the sea. It starts to gather at my feet and I notice the first of our catch: tiny, quivering fish that have speared themselves through the holes of the fine-meshed net. At first I try to pull them free and throw them into the main net, but there are too many of them and they are doomed to dry out on deck or be minced by the winches. The fisherman demonstrates how to use a foot to shove the net that has collected on the deck to the side, keeping everything shipshape. I nod to confirm my understanding.

The second boat is mirroring our actions at the far side of the net and slowly, as both boats bring in more and more, the two vessels get closer and closer together. Eventually there are just a few metres of net and a lot of fish between us.

We can now see our haul: thousands of fish, skitting around in a frenzy, probably just realising that their world has suddenly got incredibly small. As we pull in the last few inches, the water boils as the panicked creatures leap into the air and thrash on the surface. A few do manage to soar to safety and swim another day, but for most there is no escape. The net is now taut between the two boats, the fish consolidated into a struggling mass of silver. Dawn is spreading as one of the crew swings a tiny boom crane out and over the net and begins to scoop up our catch. The crane's net bulges with fish as he swings it back over the boat and dumps the haul into ice-filled holds.

Once emptied, the crew reset the net and we chug off to repeat the process on a second. By the time we have emptied it, our boat is sunk low in the water. Fully loaded, we begin to make our way back to Obama, heading directly for the fish market.

'Jerry, is it a good catch today?' I ask.

'Yes. Good catch. You must bring luck!' he replies, smiling. He translates for his crew mates and they nod in agreement.

The grey dawn is diminishing and daylight is beginning to appear. Our captain, who has close-cropped salt-and-pepper hair, opens an ice hold, reaches in and pulls out two large fish and a squid.

'Can you eat raw fish?' asks Jerry.

It always struck me as a strange question but I had been asked it many times before. The phrase made it sound as though eating raw fish was a special skill rather than a personal preference. Optimum breakfast time for me was still some way off, but I reply truthfully:

'Yes. I can eat. I like.'

The captain beckons me to watch as he places the catch, still live, on a large wooden chopping board and picks up a knife. He removes the guts and head then expertly fillets the fish that just minutes ago had been swimming in the Sea of Japan. He cuts several thin, boneless slices, pours some soy into a small bowl and adds a curl of *wasabi*. The squid is dispatched with equal speed, its insides thrown overboard where the swirling mass of gulls fight for it. To accompany this *sashimi* breakfast, the captain produces a large plastic bottle of whisky and fills some glasses. Then he cracks open two cans of beer.

I raise a toast to the fisherman of Obama bay: '*Campai*!'

'*Campai*!' the crew reply with a smile, knocking back their whiskies in one go.

I glance at my watch: 6:15am and we have started drinking already.

'Jerry, do you have whisky and *sashimi* for breakfast every day?' I ask.

'Oh yes Sam *san*, every day. This is a fisherman's breakfast. Good *ne*?'

It was good. In fact, it was the finest, freshest *sashimi* I have ever tasted and the setting wasn't bad either. As it was now light, I could see the lush forested mountains that wrapped the bay, shrouded in soft morning mist. Craggy cliffs topped with trees watched over us and floating fishing platforms with red and yellow umbrellas bobbed on the smooth waters.

'Sam *san*, why do you come fishing with us?'

The question came from the captain, via Jerry, in a blend of English and Japanese.

He explained that his crew found it hard to fathom why two foreigners, two *sensei* even, would want to come and work on a fishing boat for free. Teachers are held in high regard in Japan and this was unusual behaviour. The crew nodded at my explanation of 'meeting new people' and 'seeing new things' but seemed to remain slightly puzzled.

We approached the harbour. People were busy ferrying boxes of crabs and fish from boats to a warehouse. After the relaxing ride in, it was time for action again. We hopped from the boats to the harbour side and set to work unloading our catch.

Using another little crane, the fish were scooped from the ice holds and dumped onto waist-high wooden trays whence the sorting began. My crewmates were fast to identify and sort the fish into different boxes. Some species were easy to tell apart but some looked identical to my eye and I had to double check to ensure I put them in the right place. It took us a good hour to sort the catch, which was then immediately taken to the auction warehouse on the quayside, where restaurateurs and fishmongers placed their bids.

It was enlightening to see the entire process from start to finish but I was struck by the phenomenal amount of fish that was wasted. By the end of the sorting process, I was literally shin-deep in small, dead fish. Thousands of small fry – fish ranging from 5cm-10cm – were simply swept onto the floor, hosed down into the drains and back into the sea. It was a complimentary breakfast for the bickering gulls and hawks that were now swirling around us. If such terrible wastage is being repeated in every fishing village across Japan and the rest of the world, it's little wonder that global fish stocks are plummeting. I wondered why such a fine-meshed net was used when the small fish that it ensnared were discarded.

But Japan's appetite for fish is voracious. The Japanese make up around 2% of the world's population, but consume about 10% of the world's catch. Domestic fisheries can't land enough to feed demand so 40% has to be imported. Their consumption of marine life is so great that Japan has become a target of overfishing campaigners and is blamed for posing the greatest threat to the future of the world's fish stocks.

At the centre of the dispute is the *maguro* or bluefin tuna, the nation's most highly prized fish. Valued for its delicious taste and texture, *otoro* (a fatty cut from the tuna's belly), is one of the most expensive dishes on the sushi menu. Both the Southern and the Northern bluefin are critically endangered, whilst the Pacific bluefin is classified as threatened and vulnerable. But as it becomes rarer, the price simply gets higher meaning there's always big profits for those involved in the industry.

Japan's fisheries, and more significantly other countries that sell to Japan, are reluctant to stop the trade in a fish that has fetched more than $170,000 per carcass. Pressure from the international community to reduce or cease fishing for endangered species is not generally well received in Japan, with retorts that such calls are anti-Japanese and culturally insensitive. However, Japan has cut the size of its commercial fishing fleet, reduced its number of factory boats and there are initiatives to encourage line-caught tuna and other sustainable fishing methods. But environmental organisations urge that global fish stocks are still at great risk if more is not done to crack down on overfishing.

By 8:30am, our catch had all been sorted and sold. Captain seemed happy; it was a good haul and had sold at a good price. We graciously accepted a box of fish called *sawada* as an *arigatou*, even though we knew there were far too many and that we could never eat them all ourselves.

I slipped out of my overalls and boots and returned them to Jerry who hosed off the fish scales. As we drove back to Ryan's home, weary, with yawns creeping in as the whisky buzz wore off, Jerry passed on a kind compliment from the captain.

'My boss like you. He say you have wide mind.'

We thanked Jerry, said our goodbyes and settled down to a breakfast barbecue of *sawada* as the heat of the day began to build.

***

Had it not been for a certain president of the United States, the tiny town of Obama would still be as I left it; a sleepy fishing port, known for nothing other than a tragic abduction, some twenty-five years previously.

On the 7th of July 1978, Yasushi Chimura, then 23, left his home to go and meet his fiancée Fukie Hamamoto. He never came back. His small truck was later found with the key in the ignition at an observatory near the shore. The couple had been kidnapped by North Korean agents.

During the late 1970s, a number of Japanese were abducted from various locations on Japan's west coast, supposedly to teach Japanese language and culture to North Korean spies. Seventeen are officially known to have been kidnapped, though as many as eighty are suspected to have been taken. I later visited a plaque that sits on a lonely road overlooking Obama bay and commemorates this awful incident. In 2002, twenty-two years after they were stolen, the couple were finally returned to Japan. Many of the others were not so fortunate.

Thankfully, Obama was to win much happier notoriety. During the US presidential elections of 2008, the residents of this sleepy fishing town decided to pledge their allegiance to Barack Obama. But it wasn't his policies for change they approved of, nor the fact that he would make history by becoming the USA's first black president. No, the people of Obama just thought he had a good name.

It all started in 2006 when Barack visited Japan. Upon seeing his passport, the immigration officer mentioned that Obama was his home town. Local reporters ran the story, prompting the mayor of Obama to send Mr Obama a pair of Obama-made chopsticks and a letter wishing him luck in the election. Mr Obama sent a reply thanking the people of Obama for their support, which fuelled Obama fever even further until Obama-mania gripped the town. 'I love Obama!' T-shirts were printed; 'Go Obama!' flags were flown; sweet cakes called *manju* featuring

Obama's face went on sale; as well as Obama burgers and Obama *sushi* rolls.

When Obama won, Obama rejoiced. The town gathered and cheered in the streets, the 'Obama Girls' dance troupe twirled the hula, and the 'Anyone Brothers Band' performed their tribute song 'Obama is Beautiful'. There has even been talk of a statue of the president being commissioned in his honour.

At one time, fishing had been Obama's main industry. But as Jerry had explained, now just a handful of boats operated out of the harbour. Tourism has taken over and, due to an unlikely coincidence, Obama the president has helped revive this ancient fishing port, bringing in much needed visitors. And Obama the town is only too happy to welcome them.

Chapter 17
Festival Fever

Japan loves a festival. If there's something to be celebrated, then celebrated it will be. No village is too small to throw the party, no subject too strange (or mundane) to venerate. There are *taiko* drumming festivals, fire festivals and fighting festivals. There are festivals to celebrate the spring *sakura* (cherry blossom), the changing of the autumn leaves, and the heavy snows of winter. Every year in Okayama, 9000 men wearing glorified g-strings gather to celebrate *Hadaka Matsuri* – Naked Man Festival. In Kawasaki, a giant willy is paraded through the streets for *Kanamara Matsuri* – Festival of the Steel Phallus. But it was one of the newer additions to Japan's festival programme that I was most excited about, and the time had finally come to venture there.

The school term was coming to an end. But although lessons were over, club activities would continue throughout the summer, so for the students and other teachers, there was little in the way of a holiday. For me, however, it meant eight weeks off and the chance to explore more of Japan. I was kick-starting my summer with a trip to the Fuji Rock Festival.

Fuji Rock is a massive, three-day music festival held on the mountainsides of Naeba in Niigata prefecture. Having spent a series of summers in my teens and early twenties at music festivals, I was keen to see how Japan's take on live outdoor music, collective camping and the Portaloo experience would compare.

The first, and most painful difference, was the price; it cost almost twice as much as a ticket to Glastonbury Festival, and was by far the most expensive music festival I'd been to. But then it was also the only music festival in the world where you could take a ski lift to the chill-out zone.

I had recruited a team of equally enthusiastic friends and we had booked our tickets months in advance. Now the day had arrived.

'Tents?'
'Check!'
'Tickets?'
'Check!'
'Beer?'
'Check!'
'Bags?'
'Check!'
'*Ikimasho!* Let's go!'

We had hired a Jeep Cherokee from the local 'fixer' – Hiro. A man of many talents, Hiro could count engineer, property mogul, mechanic, car dealer and dance entrepreneur amongst his occupations. He ran regular salsa nights called 'Doctor Salsa' from his 'Salsa Lab' and had a nice sideline selling cars to Fukui's foreigners.

My Fuji Rock team consisted of Lewis, an exceptionally English man; Ruan, a slender South African; bearded Jesse from New Jersey, and my Tennessean beach bum friend Ryan. As the heat of the August day began to gather, we piled into the Jeep, fired up the engine and set off with excitement towards Niigata.

Up and out of Fukui we drove, along the rocky coast of Ishikawa before swinging inland, chopping off the Noto peninsula and entering Toyama prefecture. In the distant east were the ever-present mountains; to the west were flat plains. We passed through various towns and sprawled settlements. The highway weaved through paddies and swung by more peaks, nearing the coast as we crossed the border and entered the long, stretched prefecture of Niigata.

Fuji Rock was founded by a man called Masahiro Hidaka. He had attended England's Glastonbury Festival in the mid '80s and was so enamoured with his experience that he took the concept back to Japan. At that time, Japan simply wasn't ready for such a large scale event; but Hidaka knew there was a market for it and eventually established the

Fuji Rock Festival in 1997, so-called because it was held close to the base of Mount Fuji. But at that very first event, disaster struck.

The festival was battered by a typhoon, devastating the site and leaving no other option but to call the whole thing off. It seemed the spirits of Fuji Mountain were not happy with the invasion of their sacred land. Years of planning were ruined and Hidaka's dreams were washed away along with the rest of the festival site. But Hidaka and his company didn't give up. They regrouped and the following year relocated the festival to a temporary site near Tokyo whilst looking for a more permanent home. Now held on the grassy slopes of Naeba 'Ski and Golf Resort', Fuji Rock Festival is Japan's premier music event, attracting the biggest names in Japanese and international music and some 100,000 fans each year.

We were still a couple of hours away when we pulled into a service station and I initiated the 'spot the festival-goer' game, a sport of which I consider myself to be a premier league player, with some ten years of experience under my belt.

'Those guys are definitely going,' I said to Lewis, nodding towards a group of young, tattooed Japanese men who looked the festival type.

'Could be...' Lewis agreed, noting the skate punk uniform of shin length shorts, white socks and baseball caps.

I strolled over and asked in Japanese:

'Excuse me, are you going to Fuji Rock?'

Their reply was affirmative. And not only were they going to the festival, but they were members of a Japanese ska-punk band called *Kemuri* who were actually playing there. We all shook hands and promised to come and watch the show.

'I get bonus points for that one,' I said as we pulled back onto the road, warmed by the encounter, which had served to fuel our festival excitement even further.

A little more than an hour later we reached our final destination: Yuzawa, a small town at the base of Naeba ski resort. Yuzawa had a frontier feel to it. The wooden shop fronts were almost spaghetti

Western: worn and slightly tired. During Japan's ski boom in the '80s the town had thrived on tourist yen but when the bubble went bang, visitor numbers fell; and though it's still one of Japan's best ski resorts, its days of glitz seemed to have passed.

On Yuzawa's main strip, crowds of festival-goers sat in the shade on their bags and boxes of beer. As we neared the main gates, we were approached by ticket touts. Like all big events around the world, touts like to get a slice of the action. Unlike other big events around the world, these ticket touts were touting their tickets at face value. We passed on their very reasonable offer, moved through the entrance and followed signs for the 'Wristband Exchange Place', switching our tickets before heading deeper into the site.

Up ahead we spotted a huge queue. Hundreds of backpacked Japanese still laden with tents and camping gear were making a beeline for one stall. As we neared we saw it was selling Fuji Rock T-shirts and other official merchandise. Perplexed that people were waiting in line for an hour before the festival had even begun just to get a T-shirt, we walked on by, forgoing the obvious 'must have' of the weekend.

The Naeba Ski Resort and Golf Course is set amongst forested mountains. Ice cold streams rushed down through dense undergrowth. Grassy trails meandered up high into the hills. It was a beautiful setting for a festival, but we discovered that ski resorts do have their downsides when it comes to camping. Finding a flat pitch is one.

'Let's keep going,' I suggested as we passed tents that had been set up on giant slalom ski runs. Possessions bulged from their sides as gravity took its toll. A flat spot that was still vacant appeared up ahead but as we neared, we were confronted with a hand-painted sign written in both Japanese and English:

'This is a LADIES camp area. Only LADIES are allowed to sleep over. Else over there.'

'LADIES' was also underlined in red, so they were serious.

Seeing as we were not LADIES, and therefore would not be allowed to sleep over, the search for flat space continued. We moved deeper into the busy campsite and were finally rewarded for our perseverance, finding a suitable horizontal spot. We set to work claiming our stake and our camp began to take shape. We had brought a gazebo to act as a communal shelter, as well as folding chairs, rugs and mats. But as everyone's tents were nearing erection, Ruan was still rifling through his bags with increasing panic.

'Oh shit!' said the South African. 'There are no poles!'

'What! You didn't check?' said Jesse who was, in theory at least, Ruan's tent mate for the weekend.

'It's not my tent! I just borrowed it,' retorted Ruan.

'Anyone got a spare tent?' asked Jesse.

It was a schoolboy error, but with some adjustment to the sleeping arrangements, we managed to accommodate them in alternative tents.

We had picked a good spot. We even had a 'garden', the putting green of the seventh hole, which was off limits to campers. It occurred to me how obedient the Japanese campers were. Had this been in Britain and a group of lager-swigging lads had been presented with the choice of:

a) camping on a ski slope, or

b) camping on a lush, soft, perfectly flat, manicured putting green, guarded only by a single piece of rope and a sign politely asking people to refrain from pitching there…all 18 holes would have become prime real estate for the weekend.

But here in Japan, this was not the case. Admirably, that polite sign and single rope was enough to keep the greens free from encroaching tents. Nobody, not even the foreigners present, pitched up on these precious oases of flatness, in the predominately off-horizontal landscape of blue, red, and double black ski runs.

Now established, we could relax. Cracking open cans of Asahi beer, we looked around us. In the valley below, layers of mountains, each one fainter than the one in front, disappeared into the distance. We watched streams of excited festival fans pour in, all trying to find that little bit of space to camp.

We spent the rest of the day wandering. The humidity rose as the hours wore on, eventually resulting in a downpour. We dashed for the gazebo, enjoying its shelter as huge, tropical drops splashed down. Having attended some of Glastonbury Festival's wettest, muddiest years, the rain did little to dampen our spirits but it did turn many of the grassy paths into mud. The storm soon passed, the clouds cleared and the sun burned again for another few hours, before sinking below the mountains, casting the campsite into shadow.

Come nightfall, we were treated to an extravagant display of fireworks to celebrate the opening of the festival, followed by a slew of bands playing in one of the marquees. We danced into the night with hundreds of other excited music fans, before heading back to camp.

Whereas the campsites at UK festivals are centres for mischief, mayhem and much high-jinks, here it was all remarkably civilised, with seemingly little going on after lights-out. Campfires were not permitted, which definitely dissuaded campsite congregations. Or perhaps it was just out of respect that the Japanese thought campsites were for sleeping in, not partying in. Either way, I felt that this was one important element of festival life that was lacking. But it did mean that you didn't get woken in the night by people drunkenly collapsing onto your tent.

***

I awoke at 7am when I could no longer bear the heat of my tent. As soon as the sun burst over the mountains, our shelters were transformed into nylon greenhouses. I unzipped my door and was greeted by a beautifully clear blue sky, framed by forested peaks. The others were stirring and Ryan, who in his typically carefree nature had not bothered to bring a tent at all and had slept in the gazebo, was already up. We fired up a camp stove and were soon slurping down instant noodles for breakfast.

One of the benefits of camping in a ski resort was the streams and rivers that rushed down the hillsides. As the heat of the day began to build, Ryan and I wandered up the mountain side for a cooling dip. The water was ice cold, the perfect cure for the heat. We dunked our head towels and T-shirts and headed off to start watching the bands. The stages were situated on flatter ground at the base of the slopes, amongst lush coniferous forest, which was shrouded in soft mist. We wandered through forest paths, passing bizarre sculptures and glitter balls suspended from bamboo poles. Further on we came to the aptly named 'Place of Wonder', where immense sculptures made from VW Beetles and other junkyard scrap towered high.

That was much excitement in the air. We were all music fans but New Jersey Jesse loved live music the most. He had planned his weekend to see as many bands as possible, ensuring he could enjoy the music from the first band to the very last. Once in front of a band he liked, he entered a kind of trance, grooving away all day long. But after the first night, Jesse began to complain of an inflamed spot on his leg. Our Fuji Rock information packs had warned against snakes, mosquitoes and bears. There were certainly mosquitoes in the dusk air, which are endemic across Japan for much of the year, but Jesse had been bitten by a tick, which caused his leg to swell up and required medical attention.

Aside from the pesky bugs, most festival-goers at Fuji Rock were very well behaved. Amazingly, I barely saw a single piece of litter on the ground for the whole weekend. Recycling points and portable ash trays, combined with the Japanese ability to follow rules, meant that the clean-up crews would have little to do once the festival was over. Every other festival I have attended is, by the end of the event, a sea of burger boxes, beer cans, and chip wrappers.

Drugs were also very obviously absent. Anyone attending any of the big festivals in the UK would find it impossible to avoid the call of the passing drug dealers offering their wares: 'Skunk! Mushrooms! Speed! Pills!' In comparison, the closest I came to any illicit substances over the four-day period was a faint whiff of marijuana drifting on a breeze. I tried to locate the source, but they had long since melted into the crowds.

Japan's drug policy is very strict; there is no classification between hard and soft; possession of cannabis is a very serious offence, and during my two years in Japan, drugs never crossed my path. Every now and then you heard rumours and stories of foreigners being caught, doing jail time and getting deported.

Because the penalties for drug convictions were so severe, I had been surprised to see that several of my 13-year-old students had pencil tins with bizarre drug-related designs.

'Be arrested on a marijuana possession charge. I am from Jamaica' said one that was illustrated with a big cannabis leaf on top of a Jamaican flag. Another read:

'Reggae Monkey. Bogart the joint!' and pictured a chimp wearing a Rastafarian hat smoking a huge cannabis cigarette.

But rather than being a symbol of rebellion as in the UK, where cannabis-leaf-emblazoned T-shirts and posters have become part of the teenager's uniform, I discovered that the kids here were completely oblivious as to what a 'joint', 'marijuana' or 'cannabis' were – let alone the definition of a 'reggae monkey'.

One of the aspects of music festivals that I have always enjoyed is meeting new people. Over the weekend we managed to engage with many of our neighbours. I befriended a heavily tattooed couple a few tents over, who permitted me to take pictures of their impressive body art. Ryan met two Japanese girls who seemed somewhat enamoured with the American and were to spend much of the weekend with us. We also met a girl called Miki who had made the five-hour journey to Fuji Rock for just one day, so she could see her favourite band; she would catch the last train home. When we expressed surprise, Miki explained:

'Many Japanese people do this. It is quite normal.'

Indeed, travelling long distances for short periods does seem to be a common practice in Japan, and I later found out that going to Australia – a nine-hour flight – just for the weekend was not unheard of.

***

We spent the three days of the festival amongst packed crowds watching bands, boogying to DJs and generally having a great time. We saw all sorts of acts, from the big headliners like the Foo Fighters, Fat Boy Slim and Beck to obscure Japanese performers of which we'd never heard. And we managed to catch Kemuri, the ska-punk band we had met on our journey, who played a fast set to an energetic crowd.

Being such a massive musical event, Fuji Rock attracts many Westerners. But I am ashamed to say that there were a few who made me ashamed to be Western, and in particular English. Most memorable was Ziggy.

We were sitting on the grass in front of the main stage, enjoying the sun and an Asahi beer, when we saw him coming. A twenty-something guy, he ambled through the crowd with a Noel Gallagher-style sun hat, and the same arrogant swagger. Then, spying a pretty Japanese girl, he strode right up to her and with barely an introduction, started to touch her hair. She tried to back away in the politest possible way, but he advanced and then unbelievably, tried to kiss her. She was clearly uncomfortable and had this been back in England, Ziggy would have likely received a slap round the chops for his trouble.

But it was evident that this was familiar territory for Ziggy and he knew he could get away with it. The poor girl eventually managed to fend him off, at which point he just shrugged as if to say 'plenty more where she comes from', spotted us and invited himself to sit down. I immediately disliked him.

Whenever two Westerners meet for the first time in Japan, there is usually some sounding out, a bit like two male peacocks during mating season. They circle each other, sizing up their opponent, seeking to establish the dominant male. Who has been in Japan longer? Who is more knowledgeable on the local culture and customs? Who speaks the lingo better?

After establishing nationality, place of residence in Japan and job, the inevitable question to be asked is:

'How's your Japanese?'

To this, with great pride, Ziggy announced:

'Been in Japan for three years. Don't speak a word!'

Ziggy was a breed that I had largely managed to avoid. Making no effort to learn any Japanese, they spend their time drinking with other foreigners and moaning about Japan. The only Japanese people they speak to are the girls they are sleazing on, and they take great advantage of the enhanced pulling power about which I've already written.

A few hours later, we had another run-in with an arrogant Englishman. We were queuing for the sinks where a long line of Japanese punters were patiently waiting. A twenty-something guy appeared, took one look at the queue, then pushed straight to the front. We decided to draw his attention to his rudeness.

'Mate, there's a queue here.'

'So?'

'So get to the back like everyone else.'

'Fuck off!'

A minor slanging match ensued but alas, the queue-jumper didn't repent his queue-jumping ways.

It was another sad example of Westerners taking advantage of the Japanese passive nature, safe in the knowledge that repercussions were unlikely to be forthcoming.

***

After four days of ska, reggae, rock, rap and rave, not to mention scant sleep and much boogying, we were weary. Packing our gear into the Jeep, we left Naeba, and began the long drive back to our beloved

Fukui. It would be just a temporary stop over. The summer was still young, and I had plans to escape the heat of Honshu and flee Fukui's harshest season with a road trip to Japan's far north.

Chapter 18
Slow Boat to Hokkaido

Fukui, and indeed much of Japan, suffers from unpleasantly hot and humid summers. Tarmac softens underfoot and distant mountains disappear in a haze. Wandering outside of air-conditioned zones is ill advised; even a slow stroll to the local *conbini* store results in the uncomfortable union of shirt and skin.

I had already experienced a sauna of a summer when I first arrived in Japan. Stepping from Narita Airport's cooled climate to collide with a wall of ferocious heat had been a welcome too warm for my liking. Coming from cool Britannia, where three consecutive days of dry weather during June, July or August constitutes a good summer, it had been hard to adjust.

This time round, the onset of the heat had been more subtle. After a pleasantly warm spring, the summer had built gradually, week by week. As the sunlight hours grew, the air slowly became a little wetter, a little warmer and a little heavier until it began to stifle, its choke tightening by the day. It eventually became so weighty that it was like a soup; so hot and thick it was an effort to breath. And then came the rains.

'Sam *san*, Japan has four seasons,' I was frequently reminded by my Japanese friends.

But that's not quite true; it actually has five. What the tourist propaganda fails to mention is the *tsuyu* – the rainy season. Starting in early June, it's the black sheep of Japan's seasons. Siberian fronts collide with warm southern air, resulting in several weeks of heavy, tropical storms that sweep up from the Okinawan islands and head northwards. It's a time when most people stay indoors, hotels drop their rates and tourist hot spots are deserted.

The intense humidity was difficult to deal with. It's bearable when you're in a T-shirt, shorts and flip-flops, but sitting at my desk in a collar and polyester trousers when it was thirty-three degrees centigrade and the air was 95% water was no fun at all. It had a terrible effect on the students, and other teachers too. Like a bee-keeper's soporific smoke that calms his swarm, the humid air sent everyone into a docile stupor. No-one wanted to be sitting in a horrible, hot, humid room. Me included. The classrooms had no air conditioning, and even though their giant windows were slid right open, the thick, still air offered no hope of a breeze.

The staff room *was* equipped with an AC unit. But was it switched on? No. The culture of endurance – *gaman* – the thing that had impressed me so much during the sports day typhoon, had now become a curse. One flick of one switch would have made everyone's working day infinitely more pleasant. Instead, everyone walked around repeating the mantra: '*Atsui yo, Atsui!* (It's hot! It's hot!)', wafting themselves with promotional plastic fans bearing the brands of mobile phone or car companies. Our environment was being ignored. School rules were overriding common sense; the AC must remain off until we had melted into a pool of our own sweat.

It was around this time that the Japanese government was spending billions of yen promoting its 'Cool Biz' campaign. In an effort to reduce electricity consumption by AC units, Japan's workforce were being encouraged to take part in a radical, ground-breaking new movement that challenged all current ways of thinking.

The concept? When it was really hot and humid, people should wear clothes better suited to really hot, humid weather and turn the AC down. Heavy suits and long-sleeved shirts were out; breathable fabrics and shirts with short sleeves were in. Ties were to be ditched altogether and undoing your top shirt button was to be made a socially acceptable practice.

I hated the humidity of the *tsuyu* but I did have a deep appreciation for the Japanese rain. The earthy smells, the moody grey skies, the feeling of quiet calm a day of rain would bring. The sound of big tropical drops splashing down on the tiled roof tops, a torrent streaming from a broken gutter, the cosy feeling of being indoors during a storm, or the delights of walking outside whilst warm rain battered my umbrella. Rain is one of the pleasures of life; many might disagree, but is it not better to embrace and enjoy it, rather than detest and avoid it?

More than anywhere I had been to before, I found the weather altered not only the scenery, but the emotion and mood too. Japan's seasons are ever-changing and they seemed to add a pronounced flow to life: a sense of movement. Their rhythm remains our last connection to nature where she has been shouldered out by concrete and asphalt. Their coming and passing reinforces the feeling that time is always moving on; nothing lasts forever, which perhaps helps to explain the Japanese appreciation for all things ephemeral.

***

I had no intention of suffering through another steam-bath summer, so had hatched an escape plan. I would assemble a team of experienced road trippers and head to the far north of the country. We would cross the Tsugara Strait, which separates Honshu's sticky summer from Japan's second largest and much cooler island – Hokkaido. Here we hoped to find refrigerated refuge in its deep lakes, cold rivers and snow-topped volcanoes.

Three of my childhood friends, Chris, Gary and Danny, had come over for the summer. In various combinations, we had road-tripped though Europe, New Zealand and Canada, so they were ideal men for the mission. Pointing our bonnet northwards, we exited the comma-shaped Fukui, drove into Ishikawa prefecture and then across Toyama, along numerous toll roads and through countless tunnels. The sun beamed through the windows, and the temperature inside our heavily laden Jeep began to rise.

'Can you turn the air con on?' asked Danny.

'It is on,' Lewis replied.

'Well can you turn it up then?'

'It's already on max.'

'Great. This is going to be one sweaty trip…'

We were discovering that the Jeep's capacity to keep us cool was mediocre at best. If we rolled the windows up and had the AC on, we were sweltered by hot still air, but if we turned the AC off and wound the windows down, we were blasted by hot moving air.

After five or so hours, we left Toyama prefecture, entered Niigata and headed for the coast, deciding we'd had enough driving for one day; we were sticky and desperate to get out of the Jeep. Locating a pleasant campsite right on the coast, we pitched our tents on a grassy lot, next to a young Japanese family.

A little boy came out of a rather flashy tent and stared at us.

'Hello! What's your name?' I asked.

He shot back in to his tent screaming with laughter. Then his little head edged around the door again and he came running straight at me with a *kancho*. Though I had heard much about the *kancho*, this was the first time I had been in the firing line. A common prank amongst school children, the name of the 'game' is to clasp your hands together so that your index fingers are pointing out, and then ram them up an unwitting victim's bottom whilst simultaneously shouting 'Kan-CHO!'.

Luckily I was on to him straight away, and a firm '*Dame!*' ensured my rectum was not violated. Having escaped the anal probe, we grabbed our towels and went to cool off in the sea that sat beyond a narrow, empty beach.

'Watch out for jellyfish,' I warned, unsure as to whether the official swimming season had ended yet. It seemed it hadn't or else Niigata's jellyfish had entered the wrong post code into their Sat Navs.

We lolled for a while on the sand then, sufficiently cooled, wandered back to our camp and ignited the barbecue coals. Soon the sizzle of juicy prawns and the supping of beer joined the song of the cicadas and cricket chirp. Sitting in lamp light, we discussed our options.

'We're here,' I said, pointing at the map.

'And we've got to get to there,' I continued, tracing my finger all the way up through the prefectures of Yamagata, Akita and Aomori to the very tip of Honshu, from where we would catch a ferry to Hakodate in Hokkaido.

'That looks like a long way,' said Chris.

'Could be another two, maybe three days driving,' mused Lewis.

'And the Jeep's a bit cramped.'

'And hot.'

Like all the best road trips, the idea of having anything resembling a detailed plan had been scoffed at. Now I was wishing we had paid a little more attention to the route. We had seriously miscalculated the time it would take to drive from Fukui to the northern tip of Honshu. As the summer heat intensified, we needed to get as far north as quickly as possible. It was now dawning on us that spending days crammed in a hot car wasn't going to be the excellent adventure we had hoped for. A change of plan was needed.

'Could we catch a train or even a plane?' suggested Gary.

'Too expensive. And what about the Jeep and all the gear?' I said.

'A ferry?' Lewis offered.

A quick flick through the *Lonely Planet* revealed that there was indeed a car ferry connecting Niigata and Hokkaido, and we were in luck – there would be a ferry leaving the next day! It was the perfect solution. We could all hop aboard and, in exchange for eighteen hours of sea breeze and salt spray, we would be in Hokkaido.

The next morning we arose early, said '*sayonara!*' to *kancho* boy and his family and headed to the tourist office to book our ferry tickets. We were delighted with our new plan and couldn't wait to get on board. But our smiles soon faded.

'You want a ticket? Today? I'm sorry but the ferry is fully booked,' said the lady at the desk, amazed that anyone would expect a ticket at such short notice.

'It is *Obon* week,' she reminded us.

In our haste, we had neglected to take this into account. *Obon* is a major holiday in Japan, when millions of people across the country return home to tend their ancestors' graves and celebrate with their families. It's one of the busiest times to travel and the ferry had probably been booked up months in advance.

Our hearts sank. There was now no other option but to get back into the sweat box of a Jeep, and spend another two, maybe three days driving north. Our road trip was turning sour. But then Danny had an idea.

'Let's just turn up at the ferry port anyway. There's bound to be a cancellation.'

Danny's dad had been a trucker and Danny explained that he had never booked a ferry journey in his entire trucking career. Lewis and I didn't share Danny's confidence. We'd lived in Japan long enough to know that things didn't usually work the way they did back home.

'Danny, this is Japan not Europe. Things here run like clockwork, people don't change their plans at the last minute,' said Lewis.

'He's right Danny. If they say there's no space on the ferry, then there's not going to be any space on the ferry, end of story,' I glumly agreed.

But Danny persisted with the idea and, seeing as we were out of options, we decided it was worth a shot, even if just to prove to Danny how organised and dependable the Japanese really were.

So we drove to the ferry terminal and headed for the booking office. It was here that the limitations of our Japanese became apparent. Though both Lewis and I had been learning the language over the past year, we had a tough time trying to explain our situation to the middle-aged women behind the desk.

'Hello, we would like to go to Hokkaido please.'

'Very sorry, but there are no tickets left. The ferry is fully booked. Very sorry.'

'Yes, but maybe, ferry people cancel?' I said, my Japanese crude and malformed.

'No, the ferry is not cancelled. It is running perfectly on time and will be leaving in four hours.'

'Yes, but maybe some people cancel?'

'No, the ferry will not be cancelled.'

'Yes, we understand, but tickets…we buy cancel tickets?' tried Lewis as I desperately searched the phrasebook, trying to find the right words.

'You would like to cancel your tickets?'

'No no! We, er, we want to buy cancel tickets.'

'I'm sorry, there are no more tickets. This is *Obon* week. Very busy. All tickets have been sold. Very sorry.'

'Yes, but, maybe some people don't come to ferry? People don't go on ferry, so, er, we go on ferry?'

There was a slight flick of comprehension about what the rather stupid, disorganised foreigners might be trying to say. After a quick consultation with her colleague she said:

'Ah, you want to wait for a ticket cancellation?'

'Yes! Yes please!'

There was much inhaling through closed teeth and some shaking of heads.

'Very sorry. This is *Obon* week. It is very busy. Fully booked. Very sorry.'

'Yes, but maybe there is a chance?'

More inhaling through closed teeth.

'How many people?' she asked.

'Five,' we said. 'And a car.'

The car part caused the most sudden and prolonged inhalation so far.

'OK, you may wait.'

So wait we did. We sat down on white plastic chairs in the small office which was aged with nicotine. An hour passed: no cancellations. A faded poster of a ferry with Japanese ladies on deck, their hair blowing in the cool sea breeze as they sailed to Hokkaido rather than sitting in a hot car, taunted us.

A second hour passed: no cancellations. We started resigning ourselves to the fact that our hair would never blow in the sea breeze like the hair of those Japanese ladies on deck. But then, with less than two hours to go before the ship was due to sail, to my great surprise (and perhaps the ferry woman's too), we were summoned to the desk.

'We have a vacancy. Please board now. Enjoy Hokkaido.'

Overjoyed, we manoeuvred the Jeep into the belly of the ship, sucking in that familiar ferry smell of diesel and car fumes as if it were the world's finest perfume.

Danny's trucking tip had paid off.

***

Being on a low-yen budget, we opted for the cheapest form of accommodation, a communal *tatami* room. Down in the guts of the ship, it was a large room covered in rice-straw mats, where twenty strangers slept side by side on the floor. Shoes had to be replaced with slippers at the door and a thin blanket and tiny oblong pillow were provided for each passenger. It was here we met some of our fellow passengers: two middle-aged truckers and a young student who seemed keen to talk. Breaking their shy stereotype (no doubt aided by multiple cans of Sapporo beer), the first thing the student said was:

'Hello. My name is Naga. Japanese men have very small willy. But I have very *big* willy. Please to meet you.'

It was not the ice-breaker that I would have chosen, but it served its purpose all the same. The evening was spent with our new friends, sharing beer and chatting in broken Japanese and even more broken English about Japan, England and the respective size of Japanese and English willies. We eventually retired, resting our heads on our little beanbag pillows, and let the pitch of the ship loll us to sleep.

***

The next morning, we rose from our *tatami* and headed out on deck. The sea was blue and smooth, more like a sheltered pond than the open ocean. The giant diesel engines ploughed us through the waters whilst gulls swirled on thermals and dolphins arced from the calm deep. We sat on plastic loungers, enjoying the sun, rolling gently on the swell.

'This is so much better than a hot Jeep,' said Gary.

Everyone agreed. We sailed on up the coast, past Yamagata, past Akita and curled around the headland of Aomori. We read and dozed. Gary's hair blew in the breeze, just like the poster had promised. Lewis didn't have much hair to be blown, so instead he taught the others a few Japanese words whilst they tested us with his *kanji* cards. Despite being out to sea, we had not fully escaped the mugginess of the mainland, and after a lunch of *yaki-soba* (fried noodles), I went to investigate the washing facilities.

There were no private showers onboard; instead, the ferry had what is known as a *sento*. I entered a small changing room, stripped to the skin and placed my belongings in a locker. I then entered a steamy, tiled room and settled on a little plastic stool to take a seated shower.

I had been to several *onsen* and *sento* before and knew the drill. Protocol dictates you must scrub and scour thoroughly before immersing yourself into the steaming waters. I cleansed carefully then eased myself into the large, deep bath. Not for the shy, it is Japanese etiquette to bathe in your birthday suit and being the only foreigner in the tub, I was clocked by wandering eyes that were wondering if the rumours about Westerners' manhoods were true (in my case they are).

The water was hot. Very hot. But I spent a while, immersed to my chin, watching the ocean waves crash past the portholes until I could bear the heat no longer.

Passing through the narrow Tsugara Strait and rounding the stiletto heel of Hokkaido, we docked in the ugly port town of Tomakomai in the late afternoon. The pleasant warmth but total lack of humidity was instantly noticeable. For now, we had escaped Honshu's hellish summer.

***

In a country that has 128 million people but is 80% mountainous, space is more precious than *Kobe* beef. Almost every flat mile of Honshu, Shikoku and Kyushu is either rice paddy or building. Hokkaido, in stark contrast, is the last remaining oasis of nature in Japan. The second largest of Japan's four main islands, Hokkaido homes only 5% of the population. Unlike Honshu, it's a place where mountains are deemed capable of standing without concrete straitjackets, rivers are left to run free without beds and banks of cement, and there still exist vast areas of untouched beauty. Only colonised by the Japanese in the last 150 years, it lacks the ancient shrines and temples but also much of the urban sprawl that blights the rest of the country.

Just one hour's drive from the ferry port, the shore of Shikotsu Lake was our destination for the night. Arriving under the cover of darkness, we pulled up at the campsite, picked a spot under the tall pines, and pitched our tents in torch light. It was here, close to the ripple of the lake, that we were yet again shown the kindness of Japanese strangers.

Being lax with our preparations, we'd not stocked up on charcoal, thinking there would be a shop at the campsite. There was, but it was closed. So we had no way of cooking our food and we were all hungry. Next to us were a group of Japanese campers, who, judging by their extravagant set up, looked like they had relocated there permanently. I walked over to them and in stumbling Japanese humbly explained our predicament.

'Good evening, I'm very sorry to disturb you, but my friends and I have arrived late, and, well, we don't have any charcoal and the shops are closed. Could you possibly spare us just a little bit so we could cook some food please?'

No sooner had I made the request than a full scale famine-relief effort kicked into action. Our neighbours rallied round, not only providing us with charcoal but with their own barbecue, their huge gas light, shiny stainless-steel cooking implements, even several cans of beer and some of their own food too! With many deep bows and *'domo arigatou gozaimashitas'* we gratefully but guiltily accepted their kind offerings as they retired to bed and we vowed amongst ourselves to buy them a crate of beer come morning. However, by the time the sun streamed through the trees the following day, waking us from our drunken slumber, the entire family had packed up and left without trace.

A glorious sunny day showed off Shikotsu in all its glory when we arose. Japan's second deepest lake, this pristine body of water is as clear as glass and edged by volcanoes, which smouldered on the horizon. We spent a lazy day swimming in its cool waters and watching shoals of small fish dart past our feet amongst the underwater gardens. I had brought my fishing spear and suggested to Lewis that I might catch us some supper. Lewis, being a strict vegetarian, disapproved of my plan, so as the fish were rather small anyway, I abandoned it.

The following day we hiked up Tarumae-zan, a 1038-m high mountain. The guide book assured us that the peak would offer 'stunning views of the lake' but by the time we reached the top, fog had rolled in and we could barely see 100 metres, let alone the lake itself. We could however see the giant metal telecommunications equipment that topped the peak, quite clearly.

On the way back down we stopped at the little food stall. I wanted to introduce Danny, Chris and Gary to *takoyaki*, the little battered octopus balls that I had become so enamoured with so I ordered five portions.

'Without *katsuobushi* please,' I added.

Takoyaki are almost always served with *katsuobushi*, the pink shavings of the bonito fish, but I found the strong fishy flavour overpowered the taste.

The woman looked at me incredulously but heeded my request. I delivered the food to my friends who were sitting in the sun, and went back to pick up the last one. As I neared the stall I caught the old woman in the act of telling an amazing story to her colleague. It was all about a foreigner who didn't want *katsuobushi* on his *takoyaki*.

'He ordered five boxes of *takoyaki*, and then, can you believe it Sako *san*, he said he didn't want any *katsuobushi*!'

'No *katsoubushi*! On any of them? Are you sure?'

'As sure as day is day! No *katsuobushi*! That's what he said!'

'No *katsuobushi* on his *takoyaki*! Well I never heard of such a thing!'

She halted her story abruptly and looked slightly sheepish when she saw me standing at the counter.

***

After two lazy days by the lake, we headed east, inland towards Daisetsuzan Hokkaido's largest national park, situated in the centre of the island. It was a winding ribbon of a road as we climbed into the mountains but the hot weather and steep gradient proved too much for the Jeep; the radiator burst, sending out a plume of steam like a whale's blow-hole. We pulled over to assess the damage as pink radiator fluid bled onto the tarmac.

Luckily, Danny, who had been specially selected for this mission for his mechanical skills, came to the rescue. After an hour with his head under the bonnet and various trips to the public toilets for water refills, the radiator was patched up and we could continue our journey onwards.

That night we camped at the foot of Tokachidake, an active volcano. Its cone bellowed smoke and we could even hear rumbles and hissing emanating from the belly of the earth.

We all decided to hike to the peak of Tokachidake, which overlooks the fuming crater the following day. All of us, that is apart from Danny, who 'couldn't be bothered' and instead opted to spend the day sampling different varieties of cigarettes and coffee from vending machines.

Rising early, we stocked up on snacks, my fodder of choice being strips of breaded horse meat, and were soon making good progress on the barren trail. As we climbed, it occurred to me that hiking up an active volcano might perhaps not be the greatest idea ever born. What if the mighty mountain decided that today was the day to vent Mother Earth's anger? The last explosive eruption was in 1988, and its legacy is still obvious; most of the mountain was a bare, lunar landscape, devoid of flora. The orange soil and red rock, however, made up for the lack for a floral palette.

As the smoking crater loomed, billowing sulphurous toxins into the atmosphere, we passed veins of snow, sheltered in north-facing crevices. Reaching the summit after about three hours of climbing, we broke for lunch on the sun-drenched peak, before making our way back down to earth. We stopped at a crude rest hut, a way point where long-distance hikers could sleep on a raised wooden floor. We signed the little guest book and continued on our way. As we descended down a narrow ridge, the mountain showed us its two faces. On one side was terrain in which the Mars Explorer would have been quite comfortable; on the other, the green, grassy, rolling landscape could have been the Scottish Highlands.

By early evening we were back at base, where we found Danny happily puffing on a 'Seven Stars' cigarette and supping a cold can of 'Pokka Original' coffee. We lit the barbecue, cracked open cans of Asahi beer, and watched the sky ignite as the sun set over distant peaks.

***

Our last night on Hokkaido will be remembered for experiencing what Chris described as 'the very best of Japanese culture and the very worst of Japanese culture, in the space of five minutes.'

We had left the Daisetsuzan Park and were heading back west, towards the coast. Evening was approaching but we had located a campsite. We strolled into the office to book in for the night.

'Good evening,' I said.

'Good evening,' the two staff members replied in unison.

'We would like to stay one night please. We have five people and a car,' I said, readying a handful of 1000-yen notes.

The two staff members looked at each other and entered into a brief conversation. Then they turned to us and said:

'Do you have a reservation?'

'No,' I replied.

'Very sorry. But you cannot stay here tonight. You have no reservation.'

At first, I just thought we'd heard wrong. It must have just been a misunderstanding. We had mistranslated the Japanese. The three-acre campsite was completely devoid of campers, aside from a single family who were staying in two log cabins.

'We just need to stay for one night. There are only five of us,' I explained.

The staff members, who looked pained in having to tell us, said:

'Very sorry. You must reserve a place in this campsite at least three days in advance.'

Not a single tent was present. There were acres of camping space. I expressed my non-comprehension of the situation.

'I don't understand at all, you have space . . .'

But the single word reply from the staff members summed up the Japanese trait of strictly adhering to the set protocol.

'Rule.'

We left the office in disbelief. We were angry and annoyed. Darkness was gathering and there were no other campsites in the area. Where would we sleep? It was too late to find anywhere else now. But then the flip side of Japanese culture presented itself to us. The family who were staying in the log cabins had witnessed the whole scene and beckoned us over, motioning to one of their two huts. We weren't sure what they wanted but before we knew it, they were relocating grandma and the kids from one cabin and squeezing the whole family under one roof, in order to offer it to a bunch of English guys who they'd met only a few minutes before!

At first we were puzzled, but once we realised what was going on, we had to refuse their very kind gesture. It was a crazy situation; denied entry to an empty campsite due to a ridiculous rule, but then shown an incredible act of kindness, which went as far as evicting their oldest and youngest for complete strangers!

We didn't want to put this kindly family out, and we didn't want to camp in the campsite after being told we couldn't. But we had nowhere left to go, so ended up camping in the car park.

It was an uncomfortable night, gravel not being the best of bedding materials but the dark passed without incident and we rose at first light next morning to continue on our way.

***

It was evening by the time we boarded the ferry in Tomakomai and set sail for the mainland once more, leaving the cool clime of Hokkaido and heading back to the sticky air of Honshu.

We had opted for a small private room this time: four bunks and a tiny raised *tatami* area. Lewis had already donned a *jinbei* dressing gown and was teaching Gary and Chris the finer points of Japanese tea ceremony, while Danny was off smoking somewhere, so I left them to it and wandered up on to the deck. I was sad to be leaving this Japanese gem. As I plugged 300 yen into a vending machine, releasing a can of *Kirin* beer, I stared out over the calm Sea of Japan and wondered if I'd ever return to this smouldering island paradise.

'*Itsuka,*' I murmured.

One day.

Chapter 19
Of Samurai, Swords and Sushi

It was a bright day when we bowed to the sword sharpener and stepped into his beautiful wooden home. Sat under tall cedars and set amongst moss covered rocks, it could easily have been a scene from a Japanese scroll painting.

Along with a small group of friends, I had been invited to meet Umeda Shuji, a real live *togishi*, or sword sharpener. For hundreds of years, when a feudal Japan was populated with samurai, *togishi* would have been widespread. They would have needed to be, to hone the hundreds of thousands of *katana* that every samurai had the right, indeed the duty, to carry.

The *katana* sword was both a visible symbol of a samurai's rank and a tool for enforcing their status. A samurai was legally entitled to kill a member of a lower class on the spot, simply for being rude. During this period, it was the job of the *togishi* to create a deadly cutting edge that would never fail a samurai in battle (or just allow him to dish out rough justice when annoyed by a Japanese hoodlum).

But by the late 1800s, as part of huge reforms to the country, Emperor Meiji abolished the samurai's right to be the only armed force in Japan in favour of a more modern, Western-style, conscripted army. From then on, people were prohibited from wearing swords, although allowed to own them as works of art. The long era of the samurai class was brought to an end and swords lost their status as weapon of choice.

However, *katana* have remained immensely popular possessions in both Japan and abroad, and the *togishi's* role has evolved from one of maintenance alone, to being able to enhance a smith's craftsmanship by showing the lines of the blade, bringing out the grain of the steel and exposing its colour and texture, thus greatly increasing the attractiveness and value of a sword.

Today, there are fewer than 100 *togishi* left in Japan, so I felt very privileged to be visiting one, and just twenty minutes from my home. Umeda led us through his lovely house with its floors of polished wood to a small room at the side of the building – his sword room. Here a raised floor was divided by a small channel of water that flowed through the centre. Umeda, middle-aged and dressed in a white, tightly drawn *kimono*, explained that this was where he worked the blades.

At the back of the room was a rack of six swords. Below them were dozens of neatly stacked, oblong stones. Umeda shuffled to the rack, knelt, and very carefully, using both hands, lifted a sword from the rack then slowly slid away its wooden sheath, revealing its shiny steel. As Umeda spoke no English, and it was a complex subject beyond most of our Japanese abilities, Brandon, my American friend, performed the role of interpreter.

'I recondition many ancient *katana*, and also sharpen brand new blades that are made by the swordsmith,' Umeda explained.

This, we learned, was a completely separate process carried out by a master sword-maker.

'I use the whetstones to gradually sharpen and polish the metal. At each step, I use a stone finer than the one before.'

He demonstrated his method, placing one of the large whetstones onto a small wooden platform, wetting the blade in a tub of water that sat on the floor. He then leaned over the sword, applying force and rubbing it back and forth against the stone. He worked barefoot, crouched on the floor. After every few strokes he dipped the blade in the water, washing away minute filings.

'It takes about two weeks to complete each blade. When finished, it is very, very sharp,' he said.

Indeed, *katana* are legendary for their razor edge and cutting ability. Designed to slice through bone, a skilled samurai could easily remove a head, arm or leg in one cut. In Japanese film and literature, it's not uncommon for swords to halve humans at the waist, and modern tests on animal carcasses suggest this may well have been possible.

'Can the swords be sharpened by a machine?' someone asked.

'It is possible to buy machine-sharpened blades, but the quality is not so good. A true Japanese *katana* must be sharpened by hand. Only this way will create the sharpest blade and also the most beautiful.'

Umeda then picked up a wooden box that contained a collection of very fine stones.

'I use these for the last stage of the process.'

They were as thin as paper; the smallest the size of a finger nail. These would help finish the *hamon*, the elaborate, wavy blade pattern that not only reveals the quality of the sword's build but also adds aesthetic value in its own right.

I had never imagined that sharpening steel could take on such complexity but like many things in Japan, detail, precision and tradition are highly valued. In my ignorance, I had expected the process to be quick and mechanical. Now I saw that this was truly an art, and one to which Umeda had dedicated his entire life.

'The polishing expresses the true character of the sword,' Umeda went on.

'By filing away the exact amount of metal, we expose the heart of the blade. It allows us to see the quality of the smith's work, his skill of tempering and folding the steel.'

Indeed, the *togishi's* knowledge of sword construction has made them important appraisers in the quality of *katana* as well as experts in their history and styles. Umeda carefully dried the blade, returned it to its scabbard and again, using both hands, placed it back on the rack. He then selected another, more elaborately cased sword.

'This sword is 600 years old. It has definitely killed someone,' Umeda mused as he unsheathed its blade.

I wondered how many samurai hands the sword had passed through in its long life. What battles had it won or lost? Who had it cut and killed? Had it ever been used to assist in *seppuku*? A samurai performing this ritual suicide would cut open his stomach with a *tanto* (a short knife) although he was normally decapitated quickly from behind by his 'second' (a trusted friend or relative) just after the first cut had been made. This put a quick end to the samurai's suffering, while still allowing him to 'die with honour'.

Sadly, suicide is a major problem in Japan. The country has one of the highest suicide rates in the world, which can be in part attributed to the legacy of *seppuku*, the importance of preserving honour and avoiding shame. And even rural Fukui was not immune. Just a few months previous, a student of Ono High had killed himself in front of his class mates. After being scolded by a teacher for poor exam results, the boy had risen from his desk, slid open the door to the balcony, and thrown himself off the three-storey building.

But *katana* are one of Japan's most prominent icons and it's little wonder that the allure of these swords remains so strong. Whereas the broadswords of European knights have long since been relegated to medieval period dramas, *katana* continue to appear in contemporary books and films as fashionable weapons of discerning criminals. They are often depicted as being impossibly invincible, able to slice through gun barrels, trees and other swords with ease.

These days, Umeda's swords are no longer used in battle, although he believes these lethal weapons are still powerful as pieces of art.

'The power of the sword is in its beauty, because people are drawn to it. Born from sacred water and fire, a Japanese sword is imbued with human spirit,' he explained.

And he was right; people *are* drawn to these works of art. Slender, elegantly curved, with blades so shiny you could shave in them, their beauty combined with the fact that they were forged as instruments of death, designed to execute, maim and ultimately empower whoever wielded them, makes them intoxicating objects of intrigue.

We asked why Umeda had chosen to live here in Heisenji, a small rural village that sat at the foot of pine-covered mountains.

'The air must be clean and the water pristine for me to work the steel. And this is a place where you can still hear the owls hoot at night,' he replied.

'Will your children follow you into sword sharpening?' I asked.

Umeda inhaled slowly and sighed.

'It is a hard life. The work can be monotonous, lonely and uncomfortable. It takes ten years of apprenticeship before you can work alone. If they wish to learn the art, I will be happy to teach them but they must choose their own path.'

Nowadays, mass-produced blades are manufactured in their thousands in China, America and Japan. With machine etching, these replicas look little different to those created by Japan's master smiths and sharpeners, at least to the untrained eye. But it is impossible to fake a quality finish and interest in *katana* remains strong. With thousands of ancient blades that need continual reconditioning, Umeda and his fellow *togishi* should be kept busy for a long time yet.

There was one thing that just didn't quite make sense though. Umeda gave us leave to explore his house and grounds whilst he talked to a second group of visitors. Amongst his rock garden, where a fountain trickled into a small koi pool under tall cedars, we spotted an M-16 assault rifle, casually leaning against a window frame. Did Umeda's love of weaponry extended beyond the ancient to include the more modern? Or was it to protect his most valuable armoury? Perhaps it was just a child's toy. We left none the wiser.

***

After our fascinating insight into Japanese swords, we were feeling peckish, so some of us headed to one of our favourite sushi restaurants in the nearby town of Katsuyama. Because dining out was so cheap in Japan and my kitchen not well equipped for home cooking, I had taken to eating in restaurants four or five times a week.

This sushi restaurant was one of my favourites and along with my foreign friends, we gathered weekly to gorge on various types of raw fish and green tea that floated by on the conveyor belt.

The *kaiten* sushi restaurant is now well known both in Japan and abroad. Though their sushi is considered to be at the lower end of the quality scale, they are based on a simple, yet brilliant concept; customers sit around a circular conveyor belt that brings dishes past for their perusal. When you see something you like, you simply pluck it from the belt and devour it at your table. It's an excellent and efficient system, especially for those who might struggle to read a menu, because there's no need to order anything.

We took a seat and helped ourselves to a cup of *ocha*, placing green tea bags into our cups and filling them from the hot water tap at our table.

Some of the dishes that made laps of the restaurant had a Western twist. Alongside the traditional slices of *maguro* (tuna), *unagi* (eel) and *ikura* (salmon eggs) were more contemporary tastes too. And it was the beef 'sushi' which we fell so hard for. A slice of flamed browned beef, rare, tender, sprinkled with salt, sitting atop a cuboid of warm rice, it was truly divine.

Now, the smiley-faced manager of the restaurant had come to realise that, when it came to his beef *sushi*, we *gaijin* were powerless to refuse its melt-in-your-mouth deliciousness. He knew that no matter how many beef sushi he made, we would eat (and pay for) every single one.

Like a seasoned salmon fisherman might tie a fly, he carefully prepared the bait with his expert blade. Once we settled into our seats, he cast his irresistible lure onto the conveyor belt, so that it landed just a little upstream from our lair. He then waited and watched as the succulent beef trotted downstream towards us.

Upon spying his beef, we entered a feeding frenzy. Hands shot out into the slow-flowing conveyor belt current and grabbed the bait, greedily devouring it with haste. *Natto* (fermented soy beans) and *ikura* (salmon roe) were ignored, while four, five, six plates of beef sushi were gone in an instant. The master fisherman quietly smiled to himself. It was a good haul; profits would be up tonight.

Occasionally however, we piranha-like *gaijin* could cause problems for this fisherman. When another patron of the restaurant ordered beef sushi, under no circumstances could he allow it to flow past us – it would never make it through. Instead, he had to place it downstream of the *gaijin* shoal, out of striking distance.

This was however but a small inconvenience for the master fishermen. We called for the bill and the waitress scanned our stacks of plates, handing us an electronic fob, which we took to the till. As we handed over our wads of yen, he waved a friendly goodbye, safe in the knowledge that we would be back in his waters soon.

Chapter 20
Creatures of the Kuzuryu

High up in the mountain folds above Ono, there sits a lonely lake. Clear, blue-green and contained by steep, forested slopes, it was one of the most magnificent I had ever seen. But I found that my appreciation for its splendour was not shared by the locals.

They say that beauty is in the eye of the beholder. Where one culture or one person finds attraction, others may find nothing, or perhaps even repulsion. I had already noted some of the differences between Western (or maybe just my own) perception of beauty and that of the Japanese; the fact that *yaeba* (double tooth) is regarded as *kawaii* (cute) and that the pigeon-toed shuffle that many Japanese women adopt is seen as attractive because it is deemed the feminine way of walking. But whilst it's easy to understand differing views of what constitutes beauty in humans, never had I realised that appreciation for unspoilt beauty of the natural landscape could be a matter for debate.

My first inkling that the beauty of Lake Kuzuryu was not being recognised was when I tried to track down a boat in which to explore it. Had such a magnificent place been located in my home country, there would doubtless be some enterprising local offering kayaks or rowing boats for hire, capitalising on the certain demand by visitors to take to the water and enjoy its exquisite scenery. But my investigations returned no significant leads on any rentable watercraft.

'No Sam *san*, there is nowhere to hire boats. Lake Kuzuryu is not such an interesting place,' said the maths teacher.

'Boats on Lake Kuzuryu? No, I don't think so. Nothing to see there,' the sports teacher agreed.

But I had already seen that there was plenty to see. As I sat poring over a map in Yasu's bar one evening, I gazed upon the lake's numerous inlets and arms that were ripe for exploration. Looking like the cell body of a neuron, dendrites feathered from the elongated lake into hidden valleys of their own, only accessible by water.

I supped on a bottle of Yebisu beer, peeling at the label that pictured a big-eared, fat little fisherman. I had to find a way to get out there. Even Yasu, overlord of Ono's outdoor world, couldn't help me this time. So for many months, I looked upon the lake's loveliness from her banks only; she flaunted, I was taunted.

***

It was a Saturday morning as I drove up to the lake, yet again, to investigate. Along the road – the Mino Highway 158 – were a handful of long-since closed cafés and crumbling roadside restaurants. They gave the impression that the good times had been and gone. Presumably they had once enjoyed brisk trade from those who had come to marvel at the newly formed 128-metre Kuzuryu river dam, which had been completed in 1968 and had fathered the lake. Built for hydroelectricity and flood control, it had at one time been a worthy tourist attraction. But it had of course come at a cost. When the valley was flooded, over 500 homes had been destroyed, along with acres of forest and farmland.

Keiko, my Japanese 'mother', had even said that the lake was haunted; when the water level dropped, the roofs of abandoned homes sometimes appeared. I was to find that Keiko's tales weren't entirely of the old wives' variety; indeed, there was something lurking in the lake's deep waters.

I pulled in at the last surviving business along the lakeside road, a red-roofed restaurant-cum-souvenir shop. Outside there was a large sign depicting a black bear watching over the mountains. Inside, a real one – stuffed – sat above the counter. The restaurant sold 'mountain vegetables' and fish dishes, and on the wall hung a mounted trout. There were no other customers.

'Oh no, we don't have any boats. Sorry. How about a beer?' said the owner, a jolly little man with thick black glasses, who also ran a tiny campsite on the lakeside. The campsite seemed to be devoid of campers for most of the year.

'We get visitors in the summer. And in autumn people come to see the leaves turning. Yes, it's the best place in Fukui to see the autumn colours,' he said proudly, but there was an air of sadness in his tone. The days of the Kuzuryu as a 'must see' hot spot had obviously passed.

Determined to explore the lake by boat, I began looking further afield, turning to the internet for a solution. After several weeks of online research, I concluded that an inflatable 'Sea Eagle' kayak would be the perfect craft. Unable to find a Japanese supplier of the model I wanted, I ordered one from the USA.

***

A few weeks later, my parcel arrived. Having done a fully inflated dry run in my lounge, I was ready to embark on my maiden voyage. One warm day, dismissed early from work, my chance came. Throwing the kayak, a bottle of Pocari Sweat and a packet of 'Crunky' almond-centred chocolates into my car, I set off eagerly towards the lake.

I pulled into the deserted camp ground, just beyond the bear restaurant and within ten minutes, the kayak was pumped up and ready to launch. I bristled with excitement as I waded into the water. It was cool and clear, the bottom mud and rock. I hopped into the boat, slung my *tatami* flip-flops in too and began to paddle out. Finally, after months of questioning, searching and internet surfing, my adventures on the Kuzuryu could begin.

It was a warm day even up there in the mountains and just the softest of breezes stirred the surface. I paddled right out into the middle of the lake. Up ahead, a steel suspension bridge spanned the water. Named *Yume no Kakehashi* – Bridge of Dreams – it was apparently modelled on the famous Seto Bridge, which connects the island of Honshu to Shikoku. Swirls of mist hung over forested peaks in the distance. The water was a brilliant blue-green but the lake was deep and looking down into it, I could see nothing but darkness.

To my left, the wide mouth of an inlet loomed. I swung the bow of the kayak towards it and paddled on. I would explore the water beyond the bridge another day. To my right, I could just make out the signs of a logging road up on the mountainside, which ran along the inlet for a stretch, then petered out. All was silent and eerily calm. There were no people, no fish and few birds. Black, drowned trees jutted out of the water, some standing surprisingly far out into the lake. Presumably once tall pines growing from now submerged mountain ridges, their skeletons added to the sense of desertion.

I paddled further up the valley. The mountains were lush green, sheer and plunged straight into the water. I had hoped to find suitable spots for future camping trips, but there was nowhere flat enough to have a picnic let alone pitch a tent. The tree line began directly above the waterline and no lakeside paths existed. For the first time in Fukui, I felt like I was somewhere truly wild. Not a person, nor power cable, nor concrete mountainside in sight. The paradox of course was that the very lake itself was man-made.

Up ahead, the valley was widening slightly. I gazed down into the deep water and thought about what Keiko had told me. Was I paddling over the roof tops and along the streets of a sunken village? The valley cut deep and it must have been a long way down to its dark bed. I peered over the side of my boat, searching for signs of this Japanese Atlantis. And as I gazed down into the darkness, something caught my eye. I stopped paddling. The boat glided in perfect silence. I strained hard, scanning the depths. There was something down there. And it was moving. Deep down, just on the very limits of visibility, a large, dark form glided beneath me.

A sharp jolt of fear, the like of which I hadn't felt since I was standing on stage in front of the entire school about to give my introductory speech, speared me. There was definitely something there.

And it was big. A big, shadowy shape, bigger than my boat. Panicked, I strained to identify it, but the ghostly form sunk deeper and within a few seconds, it had descended out of sight.

Adrenalin coursed through my system. As someone with a strong interest in the natural world, all my accumulated knowledge told me that there were no creatures of that size living in lakes high in the Japanese mountains. So what the hell was it then? I had definitely seen something. Something larger than any creature that had any right to be in this lake.

My brain scrambled for a reasonable explanation. It couldn't find one. Then I remembered Keiko's stories: the haunted lake. Was it some sort of water demon? After all, 'Kuzuryu' translates as 'Nine-Headed Dragon'. No, of course it wasn't a nine-headed dragon. Or even a one-headed dragon. But then what could it possibly be? A giant freshwater eel? A massively mutated sturgeon? A cousin of the Loch Ness Monster perhaps?

I paddled quickly towards the bank but also as calmly as I could; I knew that large water-dwelling predators were attracted to splashing on the surface. I had also been a fool and broken a golden rule in the outdoor exploration book; I had not told anyone where I was going. If my ship went down, no one would come looking.

I kept peering into the depths, fearful of what I might see but Kuzuryu had more surprises for me yet; other things were watching me from above the waterline.

My heart was still racing as I neared the shore. Keeping close to the safety of the banks, I gathered my thoughts, still searching for an explanation. I was certain that I'd seen something but I also knew that no creatures that big could possibly live here. But I had definitely seen something. As I ping-ponged back and forth over this point, a buzzing sound, which was getting increasingly louder, snapped me back to the present.

I looked up. Coming straight at me was a massive, winged insect. The size of a small bird, its black and yellow body made an almighty drone as it homed in. It was an *oo-suzumebachi*, a giant Japanese hornet. Translated as 'giant sparrow bee', I'd never seen such a creature before though I had heard plenty about them. The world's largest hornet, its sting is said to be like a hot nail and, according to National Geographic, its venom can 'disintegrate human flesh'. Though usually only aggressive if threatened, it's reported that as many as 40 people are killed by them each year.

These are not comforting facts to recall as one of them circles you. On land, I might have had a better chance of escape (although they can fly at 25mph!) but here, out on a lonely lake, I could neither run nor hide. If this winged beast decided it was going to sink its quarter-inch hot nail into my body and disintegrate my flesh, there wasn't much I could do about it. In fact, its stinger was so big it posed a genuine danger to the integrity of my inflatable kayak. I set down my paddle leaving my hands free to defend myself and my boat.

A tense minute followed. It circled again and again, calculating whether I was a danger to its nest which, unless it had evolved gills, must have been quite some distance away. Round and round it droned, but eventually, after several laps, the creature decided neither kayak nor kayaker were a hazard, and it released me from its circle of terror, zooming away over the water. I grabbed my paddles and began a brisk stroke in the opposite direction.

Still pondering the mystery of the creature from the deep and now worrying that the giant hornet had gone to fetch his mates, I continued paddling. My blades cut through the smooth water, barely creating a ripple. The valley was now narrowing again, and the mountains, round with a thick head of forest, rose to a thousand metres or more. The boat glided silently as I looked up into the dense vegetation, which was an intense green. And up there, somewhere on the mountainside, I heard a sound: a call.

I stopped paddling, letting the boat coast. For a minute nothing stirred. I scanned the trees. Then I caught a motion: a quivering branch, a rustle. I held my breath, scouring the trees to detect movement. Then again, another branch, bouncing up and down. I watched and waited, wondering what the forest would reveal. A few more calls: animal sounds. And more branches bouncing and swaying. I stayed completely still, barely breathing. Seconds later a brown furry body and little red face appeared; it was a *saru* – a Japanese macaque monkey.

I began to paddle towards it, very, very gently, hoping for a better look. As I did, several more *saru* faces popped through the greenery. They seemed just as surprised to see me as I was them. The Japanese macaque is the only species of monkey in Japan, and is the world's most northerly living primate – apart from people. The 'snow monkeys' of Nagano, who have developed a love for hot springs, are famous, but I hadn't realised they roamed wild, here in the forests of Fukui.

I sat in my boat watching them watching me. I put in the occasional oar stroke, edging closer, and they also became increasingly more bold, climbing out onto overhanging trees to get a better look at me. Some began to jump up and down on branches, uttering high pitch screeches; a display of territorialism, a warning perhaps. I suppose kayakers, and especially foreign ones, were a rare sight in their waters.

We eyed each other for about thirty minutes. I continually glided closer with gentle paddle strokes. Occasionally one would come down from the cover of the trees and walk out onto a deadwood trunk that jutted from the bank. We each edged closer and closer to each other, until we were just a dozen metres apart. But my monkey moment came to an abrupt end; a large male, who was probably on a macho dare from his pals, made a run out onto the open bank. As he bounded down the steep rocky face towards the lake's edge he knocked some loose stones into the water. The resulting splash spooked him and within seconds the whole troop had melted back into the forest, not to reveal themselves again.

Enchanted by my meeting with the monkeys, I paddled further down this tapering inlet. The mountains were closing in, lake turning to river. My heart rate had now returned to a normal level following the sighting of the mysterious creature, though I was still puzzled about what I had seen.

The water was becoming shallower now and I could see a sandy bottom. White crags rose from the narrowing valley and the water was a turquoise blue. I was delighted with my boat; it was performing perfectly and had now brought me to one of the most beautiful places I had ever been – not just in Japan, but in my life. It was a mystery why the locals didn't make use of it. If you were to transplant a lake of this natural splendour to the UK, it would be definitely be designated an Area of Outstanding Natural Beauty. But here, no-one paid it the slightest bit of attention. Maybe the locals knew something I didn't? Perhaps the hauntings, the hornets and the creatures of the deep were keeping visitors away.

The sun sets early in the mountains, and after an afternoon of unexpected excitement I landed back at my launch point, dragged the boat up the rocky bank and packed up for the day. I had explored just one little finger of the lake, faced peril from the land, water and air, and couldn't wait to return to see what other secrets the Kuzuryu would reveal.

***

Over the next few months I took many friends out in my kayak, eager to share with them this beautiful place, which had become my own personal paradise. I took Brandon my American friend, who was very enthusiastic about the lake's good looks but who decided he needed to pee half way into the trip. We had managed to find a rare bit of flattish bank on which to land, but he had then almost capsized us trying to get back in.

Caitlin, my blue-eyed, blonde-haired American friend, was overjoyed because we had another encounter with the monkeys, and of course my girlfriend, who also loved the great outdoors, joined me many times.

I also took my mountain-climbing, bar-owning buddy Yasu out. He was one of my Japanese friends who I knew to appreciate raw natural beauty; he had no time for concrete. We had planned to go fishing and Yasu had recommended another lake nearby – Sasougawako – as a place worth looking at, so we set off for an afternoon trip.

Driving along the lush valley, through numerous tunnels, we climbed up to the mighty wall of the dam that plugged the Mana River. At the top of the dam we passed the golden statue of a woman – Princess Mana. The legend goes that she was the beautiful daughter of a rich man who once lived in the Mana Valley. One summer a terrible drought struck the village threatening to parch the crops and starve the villagers. The only way to bring rain was to sacrifice women to the local dragon. Princess Mana went willingly to her death. Heavy rainfall followed and the crops were saved.

Unlike the Kuzuryu Lake and the lake where we were now headed, Lake Managawa was less attractive. On the map it looked like a Japanese dragon – long and worm-like – and a swill of driftwood and rubbish had collected at one end. We followed the curl of the lake and then turned off onto a narrower road, close to a large, flat camping area, devoid of any campers. The road branched and became narrower still and we passed a section of mountainside that was in the process of being concreted over. This prompted Yasu to speak of his disdain for the construction projects that were blighting Fukui's landscapes.

'I hate the building work,' he said as we bumped along a narrow track, avoiding the rocks that sat on the road, having tumbled down the mountainside.

'The construction companies say it is to stop landslides. But we don't need it. It is only about money.'

I had to agree. Concrete seemed to have penetrated deep into Japan's countryside. Even up here, high in the mountains, I was amazed to see the smallest streams had been furnished with a concrete lining. Could nature ever just be left alone?

We spent the afternoon casting our lures from the kayak but the lake didn't give us even one fish. However, Yasu and I didn't really mind. We were happy just to be floating in this deserted place and Yasu was in full agreement that it was a beauty spot. Something that Yuko, my Japanese 'sister', felt very differently about.

Yuko had just graduated from university and returned to Ono to commence her career has an English teacher. She would not start full-time for a few weeks, so I invited her to join me on my kayak adventures.

Despite being an Ono local, Yuko had never made the forty-minute drive up to the lake, which I found unbelievable. But as we paddled through the deep blue waters lined by steep, forested mountains, it became apparent why; my idea of beauty and her idea of beauty were two very different things.

We paddled out in tandem, towards one of my favourite parts of the lake. Yuko had not believed me when I had told her about the little shrimps that lived there. Now, peering into the clear water, she could see with her own eyes their translucent bodies, lined with colourful veins of red. They clung to the banks, using rocks and submerged roots for cover.

We paddled on, spying a lone snake slithering across the lake's surface. For a creature with no legs, no arms and no fins, they are surprisingly accomplished swimmers.

'*Kirei neh*? (It's beautiful eh?)' I said, lost in the landscape.

But Yuko wasn't entirely in agreement. She explained that from a Japanese point of view, this place was not considered beautiful. In fact, not only was it not beautiful, but it was scary and ominous. Her reasons? Lack of people and lack of the 'human touch': exactly the same reasons that I found it so attractive.

But Yuko's words did fit with what I had already noted many times: Japan's love for 'man-made nature'. It seems somewhere can only be considered beautiful, and therefore worthy of tourist interest, once it has been manipulated and manicured by human hands. Raw, untouched, unspoiled beauty is far less appreciated. Only structured, hand-planted, man-influenced 'beauty spots' seem to make the guide books. The Japanese garden, where every piece of moss, every pebble and every plant has been carefully placed. The *bonsai*, with each branch wired into position to create the most pleasing shape possible. Even fully-sized trees in parks and gardens were pruned and preened ferociously. This human touch seems to be required before somewhere can become a legitimate tourist attraction; unspoiled nature is just the blank canvas upon which man can then create true beauty worthy of visitors.

The strange irony of this situation is that lovers of unspoilt beauty spots in Japan tend to get them to themselves. The 'must see' destinations are constantly overrun with people securing proof of their visit with photographs and *omiyage* (souvenirs) to dish out to colleagues. This leaves what I believe to be Japan's most beautiful places very much underrated and uncrowded, but also unloved.

We continued up the inlet. The water became shallower and a white sandy bed emerged. The paddles made ripples that cast patterns on the bottom and, if it wasn't for the mountainous backdrop, it could have almost have doubled for the turquoise waters of the Maldives.

As we padded onward down the narrowing valley, Yuko tapped me on the shoulder and pointed.

'Look! Down there!'

I peered into the depths. A large, dark shape was gliding below us. The creature of the deep had returned. But this time I was not scared. I had since ascertained its true identity. It was no ghost, no nine-headed dragon, no relation of Nessie. As it rose up from the depths, we could both see its true form. It was not one animal but a large shoal of carp, swimming closely together. They glided onwards, seemingly unaware of our presence.

***

Over the next few weeks, despite Yuko's initial reaction to the wilderness of the lake, we went kayaking a number of times. It wasn't until our very last trip together that she finally relented.

'OK Sam *san*. Lake Kuzuryu is beautiful after all.'

Chapter 21
Confessions of a Failed Taiko Drummer

My time in Japan was almost over. Two years had passed in a blur of excitement and new experiences. But before I left the land of the love hotel, there was a man I had to see one last time. A man of humble beginnings, he had spent the first half of his working life on a production line in a textile factory. Now he is one of Japan's leading masters of taiko – the traditional form of Japanese drumming.

I sit in the audience having just watched his performance and feel strangely nervous as I wait for his adoring fans to present bouquets of flowers and shake his hand. He graciously poses for photographs and patiently talks to everyone who approaches, yet it's obvious by their submissive gestures that he is a highly respected individual.

I feel a sharp pang of guilt as he looks up and recognises me.

'Sam san! Ohisashiburi! Long time no see!'

Such is Mr Kurumaya's enthusiasm, even for those of his pupils who had let him down.

***

I was once an arrogant student of this *taiko* drumming master. Every Saturday I had bowed deeply before stepping through the sliding door of his beautifully crafted *dojo*. The smell of pine forest wafted through the windows as he pottered around, watering the delicate orchids and creepers that adorned the room. His appearance and mannerisms reminded me of Karate Kid's mentor, Mr Miyage: especially when he spoke to me in his cryptic fashion:

'Sam *san*. Heart most important. Heart always singing.'

Known to his students simply as 'Master', Kurumaya was small in stature, big in heart. His shoulder-length hair was laced with silver and I never saw him dressed in anything other than a *jinbei*, the male version of a *kimono*. Though in his late fifties, Kurumaya's light-footed, bouncy nature suggested a man a third his age. He was a warm, charismatic character; humble, yet with such vigour for performing, it was impossible to attend his *taiko* shows without being injected with his rhythmic enthusiasm.

As a kit drummer with 15 years' experience, I was keen to try *taiko*, a traditional form of Japanese drumming, and had joined Kurumaya's *dojo* soon after arriving in Japan. I had seen live *taiko* performances in the UK and had no doubt that I could easily handle the rhythms involved. Kurumaya was delighted to have a new 'international student' and after meeting with him and talking at length, he agreed to take me on. However, it soon became apparent that I was not the devoted pupil that Kuramaya had wished for.

I had begun my training full of enthusiasm for this powerful form of percussion. I was eager to learn the correct stances, drum patterns and body movements that were all part of the art. Every week I would seat myself on the square cushion on the floor of the *dojo* and try to perform the obligatory *zazen* meditation, in silence broken only by the river that rushed past the tiny village of Mihama. I never quite got the hang of clearing my mind of all thought and, though it was a relaxing way to begin the class, my meditation skills remained basic at best.

Next we would practise the same '*ju-ichi*' rhythm over and over, clacking the thick rolling-pin sticks off the rim of the *taiko* drum as well as beating the taut leather skin. Kurumaya would watch closely with a serious expression across his brow. He would constantly scrutinise my strokes, correct my stance and adjust my grip. Each week I left the *dojo* full of energy, drumming out the new rhythms I had learned on my steering wheel as I drove home. Though I would need much training, Kurumaya must have seen a glimmer of promise in my *taiko* abilities.

'Sam *san*. One day, you can be professional *taiko* player,' he told me.

'But you must practise Sam *san*. You must work hard.'

It was a kind compliment but as the weeks went by, I began to wonder if Kurumaya's confidence had been misplaced. Despite being a proficient percussionist, I started to realise that the strong spiritual nature of *taiko*, the highly disciplined strokes and the 'all or nothing' commitment that Kurumaya insisted upon his students, were not sitting well with my desire for a casual taste of *taiko*.

I just wanted to jam out some new rhythms but Kurumaya had deeper lessons to give. He tried to teach me that there was more to *taiko* than just beating a drum. He constantly spoke of an inner energy, a rhythmic soul that needed to be tapped. Without doing so, one could never truly play.

'Sam *san*. Heart most important. Heart always singing,' he repeated, tapping his chest with his hand.

But after a few months, my attendance to his weekly classes began to wane. I started to become frustrated with the rigid nature of *taiko* that left little room for experimentation. It was all about performing set pieces rather than creating new ones. For me, drumming had always been fun but I was beginning to find *taiko* too serious. It wasn't what I had expected. As I had come to learn, like many things in Japan, there was a set protocol that had to be obeyed. Straying from this protocol was considered *chigau* – wrong. Conformity rather than creativity was encouraged. Much to my shame, I began to lose interest. I stopped devoting time to learning and rehearsing the rhythms outside of class. I was failing my Master.

***

The *taiko*, which means 'wide drum' has been around for at least 2000 years. Originally they were used as a communication tool on the battle field, to issue commands to cavalry and foot soldiers during warfare. They were also used during religious ceremonies and are still seen today in Shinto shrines and Buddhist temples. The drums range in size from the huge *o-daiko* to the small *shime daiko*. The biggest can weigh three tonnes and have a diameter of over two metres. Traditional *taiko* are made from a single piece of wood, normally a hollowed-out trunk of the Keyaki tree, which may be over a thousand years old. Master craftsmen look as much for the beauty of a grain pattern as for a wood's strength and hardness, which will influence the tone it will produce.

At the end of each lesson, we would dust down the beautiful, wooden drums, store them away and then sit in the small office that adjoined the *dojo*. The room had a record player, stacks of vinyl, an antique European clock tick-tocking on the wall, a Beatles watch and numerous other knick-knacks that Kurumaya had collected on his travels. Sipping on green tea and crunching through seaweed snacks, I would listen to him enthusiastically relate his tales from the road. He would flick through his photo albums that documented his extensive wanderings and I chuckled when he proudly pointed out his picture of topless women sunbathing on a French beach.

Kurumaya had a warm sense of humour and a kind, inquisitive nature outside of the strict confines of the *dojo*, where the atmosphere was always stern. I once mentioned that I liked a picture that was hung on his wall. He immediately disappeared, returning a few minutes later with an identical print that he presented to me as a gift.

Kurumaya was also eager to show me his vast collection of press cuttings and through these I began to piece together his life story. He had started playing music at the age of 12 and quickly became competent with bass and rhythm guitar as well as the *shamisen*, a traditional Japanese stringed instrument. In his teens he won awards for his trumpet talent whilst playing in a locally famous jazz band. It wasn't until he was eighteen that Kurumaya first witnessed a *taiko* performance, which he recalls had a profound effect on him:

'I was struck by something I hadn't experienced before. Watching the performers playing with so much energy was like catching a glimpse of an entirely different world and I immediately wanted to try it myself.'

Kurumaya was soon in love with the sound, the movements and the 'ki', or energy, expressed by this form of music. His trumpet and other instruments started to gather dust as he devoted all his spare time to *taiko*. He formed a *taiko* group and began to play live at local festivals. But in spite of his passion for *taiko*, it would be a long time before Kurumaya was to turn his drumming skills into a full-time job. For the next 30 years, from the age of 18 to 48, he continued to deepen his knowledge of *taiko*, whilst working full time at the textile factory, practising and performing live whenever he could get time off work.

His *taiko* talents grew and he began to teach the art to others in his spare time, founding a small *dojo* in a vacant apartment in Fukui city. His natural flare for performing was gaining him ever more invitations to play live and his growing reputation as a *taiko* teacher kept a steady flow of eager students knocking on his door. But Kurumaya's boss was less enthusiastic about *taiko* and became increasingly unhappy with Kurumaya's frequent absences from work. Eventually, when the chance came to tour the UK, Kurumaya said goodbye to the production line. It was a major turning point in his career, setting him on a new path. He never returned to the factory.

'Life is all about meeting people, and the most rewarding aspect of being a *taiko* player is the different people I have met and the new directions those encounters have led me in. If I hadn't taught *taiko* to the English student who came to Japan and went on to form the UK's first ever professional *taiko* group, I might never have given up my job at the factory to follow my dream of spreading *taiko* music throughout the world.'

Kurumaya's words now resonated particularly strongly with me. Doors that I could never have known even existed had opened following my decision to leave my job in England and come to Japan. The people I had met and the experiences that had enriched my life in Japan were to completely alter my career path, too. But alas, *taiko* would not be part of my future. Following my brief visit into Kurumaya's world, I was soon to step back through the *dojo* door and shut it quietly behind me. When the first snows of winter had begun to fall, the draw of the mountains had been too great to resist. It was the final nail in the coffin of my ebbing *taiko* interest; my visits to the *dojo* began to wane and eventually ceased.

My heart was singing all right but it was singing for snow and mountains, not *taiko*. Kurumaya's hopes that I might one day spread the seeds of *taiko* to new lands withered away.

Despite his deep respect for traditional ways of *taiko*, Kurumaya is most famous for pioneering new and exciting forms of music, which blend traditional Japanese instruments, such as *shamisen* or flute, as well as modern electric guitars and synthesisers with the ancient *taiko* beats. With his ever-evolving styles, Kurumaya is constantly creating new music, rather than just reciting old pieces. He has also developed a strong theatrical element to his performances, incorporating dance moves and martial art-like manoeuvres with the music so that audiences enjoy the show as much with their eyes as they do with their ears. With this innovative and pioneering attitude, Kurumaya has played a major role in the rebirth of interest in *taiko* in Japan and has been credited with transforming this traditional festival music into a highly polished and internationally respected art form. Had I persevered with my training, perhaps I would have reached the stage where I too could have been more experimental; thanks to my impatience, I never found out.

Kurumaya told me that his proudest achievements were playing live across the seas and planting the seed of *taiko* in other countries, which was perhaps why he had been so keen to teach me. Indeed, Kurumaya has performed over 300 times outside Japan – in Italy, France, Ireland, the UK and the USA – and is successfully striving to spread his own personal style of *taiko*, so that his rhythms remain alive around the world even after he has departed from it.

As my days in Japan drew to an end, I went back to the *dojo* to talk with Kurumaya one last time. We chatted long into the warm summer evening and I wondered what might have been had I been able to devote myself to his *taiko* teachings. Kurumaya had been right; heart *was* most important. And my heart wasn't in *taiko*. But if he was disappointed, he didn't show it. He seemed to understand that my heart had been stolen by other interests and seemed happy that our paths had crossed anyway. My meetings with him, though infrequent, had left me with a deep admiration for a man who had built himself up from a factory slave to an international purveyor of this art form.

Kurumaya taught me that *taiko* was more than just another drum. There is something deeper residing within this form of percussion, which requires you to play with your heart, not just your hands. It demands patience, dedication and discipline, attributes I seemed unable to apply to *taiko*. But although I never took my *taiko* to the level which he believed I could achieve, Master Kurumaya's enthusiasm, kindness and incredible energy for life lived on inside me long after I left his *dojo* and bowed to the bamboo door for the final time.

Domo arigatou Master Kurumaya.

Chapter 22
Sayonara Sadness

I cried. In front of the whole, Goddamn school. It was all going so well. I had just delivered my farewell speech in Japanese, which went fine, but when the two students who stepped up on stage started crying as they presented me with a parting gift, try as I might, I just couldn't hold back the tears.

I hope this will be by far the biggest audience to ever witness this rare phenomenon. Back when I was a student, making a teacher cry was one of the highest accolades a class of students could achieve and was seen as a triumph, though this was normally down to despicable and cruel behaviour, rather than the sadness of leaving the people and a place that was held so dear.

***

The human school friends were not the only ones I would miss. I took Shiro the school dog for a final walk today. Though she would never know it, my time spent exploring the rice paddy roads would be one of my most cherished experiences in Japan. Rather than sit at my desk and surf the net during the quiet times, I always jumped at the chance to get out and about, enjoying the simple pleasure of walking a dog.

Through heavy snow, warm tropical rain, thick sticky air and just pleasant spring sun, we had roamed the land, taking in the ever-changing scenes and smells of this beautiful locale; the mist-shrouded mountains, the bamboo thickets and the tortoises, lizards, snakes and eagles.

Many of my ideas for articles and blog posts were created and captured whilst out with Shiro, as we walked by the paddies, whether flooded to create miniature inland lakes or, as on that last day, bright and lush, accompanied by the sound of a billion rustling blades, as a breeze rippled the surface like a great green sea.

**

It was with mixed emotions that my time in Japan drew to a close. A chapter of my life was about to come to a very abrupt end and I'd be leaving in the knowledge that I'd probably never see many of these people and places again.

I found myself quite up and down about going home. Although I was looking forward to reconnecting with my family and friends, and walking once more on the soil of England, I also felt melancholy about the prospect of leaving a place that I had fallen in love with, to the point where my eyes would well up if I thought about it too hard.

Whilst many of my foreign friends had been tearing round the country trying to tick off the final 'must see' destinations, I'd been taking a more local approach, just maximising my time with the people and places that I would dearly miss on my departure.

Ironically, despite the fact that I have never been more far removed from a local population in terms of physical appearance, linguistic ability and cultural awareness, it was in a small, rural, Japanese town, considered a backwater by most, that I had felt more of a local than anywhere else in the world I'd ever lived.

Whether it was hiking through snow on some deserted peak in the Okuestu mountain range, playing football with the local team, kayaking with Yuko my Japanese 'sister' on a beautiful blue lake, or banging out some drum beats at the local bar, I had been made to feel very welcome in Ono.

The generosity and open-heartedness of the locals had made my two years very special. Shortly before I left, our 'man of the mountains' and local bar owner, Yasu, threw a little *sayonara* party for Brandon and me. It was perfect: good friends, good food and some live music performed by us all.

Brandon and I presented Yasu with a little annotated photo album entitled 'Yasu's Adventures with the *Gaijin*', which documented our snowy expeditions together. He proudly showed it off, saying it was a 'treasure'.

The last few days were a series of very sad *sayonaras*. As I packed up my life into a few boxes and bags, a stream of people dropped round to say goodbye. It was an awkward and draining few days and only emphasised all the friends I was about to lose.

***

The sun was burning hot as I loaded the final things into my car on the morning of my departure. I exchanged a one hundred yen coin for a final can of cold coffee at my local vending machine and jumped into the driving seat. I fired up the engine and was just about to pull away when Gennai, the lovable pub clown who had been ever hopeful that I would supply him with a foreign girlfriend, appeared. He presented me with a bottle of Fukui's finest *sake*. I thanked him profusely, bowed, wished him luck in the hunt for a wife and then, with a final farewell, drove out of Ono for the last time.

After two unforgettable years, my adventures in rural Japan were over.

Epilogue

There was always going to be a come down. They say it's those that don't experience culture shock who suffer from 'reverse culture shock' the worst.

In my case that was true. For two years after I returned to British soil, I thought about Japan every single day. It would just pop into my head accompanied by a little stab of sadness. Like a love lost, the happiness you once had makes it all the harder to forget. It's said that it's better to have 'loved and lost then never loved at all', but 'blissful ignorance' might disagree.

I was acutely aware of not wanting to bore my friends by recounting too many tales from Japan. I didn't want to be one of those annoying types who return from their travels only to send everyone to sleep with endless stories of their 'crazy adventures'. And, even if I'd wanted to, how do you sum up two years' worth of life over a pint?

And so I became slightly withdrawn. Where I was once outgoing, I looked inward instead. My social life suffered as I turned to my laptop and spent my evenings tapping away, rather than reconnecting with life in Britain.

Upon hearing about my experiences, some people asked:

'Sam, you got paid to walk the dog, go skiing over rice paddies and eat delicious Japanese food. Why the hell did you come back?'

Well, they say that 'paradise is a time not a place'. Whilst I don't think Fukui was quite at paradise status, my time there had certainly been the best two years of my life so far; a time when every day was an adventure into the unknown and days were never mundane.

More than many cultures, the Japanese seem acutely aware of time passing and therefore the precious, fleeting nature of it. Their beloved *sakura*, the cherry blossom, is a symbol for this ephemeral beauty, something that must be enjoyed while it lasts, because it cannot last for long.

The people I met, both Japanese and other foreigners, had all aligned like planets to provide me with a uniquely wonderful experience. But if I had stayed, things would have changed. Time moves on, people move on; what was once new and exciting becomes staid.

And so, though I do still pine for a night at Yumeya supping on *sake* and joking with Long Piece, or practising Japanese round at Keiko's house, or to be sitting on the snowy summit of an Ono mountain with Yasu, or watching giant carp cruise under my kayak in the clear Kuzuryu lake – I'll always be grateful to have been enriched by these experiences.

***

Upon my return I found my way back into the working world within a couple of months but I never returned to laboratory life. Japan had helped me to find a path I wanted to take and opened a new door. I managed to pick up employment as a writer and editor and take a new direction altogether, veering well away from both science and teaching.

I remain good friends with many of my fellow Western friends I met in Japan, and we meet whenever we can.

I'm yet to go back to Japan, but I will return.

Itsuka – one day.

THE END

Acknowledgments

Many people helped to make this book happen by generously providing encouragement, advice, feedback and editing assistance. A massive *domo arigatou* goes out to: Mike Kemp, David Parker, Jon Mitchell, my dad, my brother Al, my mum, Gareth Manning, Brandon Wright, Sam Leyton, James Ferguson, Ben Capewell and Kate Parker. And of course, I reserve my biggest thanks for the people of Ono, Fukui, Japan who made my stay such a memorable one.

If you enjoyed *For Fukui's Sake* please consider adding a short review to Amazon.

More information about the book and author can be found at:

ForFukuisSake.com

Printed in Great Britain
by Amazon